ISLANDS

ISLANDS

A trip through time and space

Peter Conrad

First published in the United Kingdom in 2009 by
Thames & Hudson Ltd, 181A High Holborn, London WC1V 7QX

www.thamesandhudson.com

British Library Cataloguing-in-Publication Data
A catalogue record for this book is available from the British Library

ISBN 978-0-500-51471-9

Printed and bound in China by Everbest Printing Co. Ltd

On the cover: A line of uninhabited cays (low-lying sandy islands,
formed on the surface of a coral reef) in the shallow waters of Chalk
Sound National Park, Providenciales, Turks and Caicos Islands.
Photo © Nik Wheeler. www.nikwheeler.com

¹ INSULARITY

Geography doles out random, inescapable fates to us. I was born on an island, which immediately determined the way I would see the world. I see that world from a distance, as if I do not belong to it – or has it perhaps expelled and ostracized me? On an island, you are disconnected, with water all around you. On an island, you are alone, even if you share the place with others. The location is by definition eccentric, because it acknowledges that there is a centre elsewhere.

For most people, islands are optional – places to dream about, the ideal site for holidays or honeymoons, times when you want to put a watery distance between yourself and a busy, vexatious reality. After you do the conscientious work of eating some food that is good for you, perhaps you earn the right to order an island for dessert. Old-fashioned French restaurants still serve up edible islands at the end of your meal: an 'île flottante' is a blob of meringue, with egg whites stiffened into volcanic peaks, that swims in a sea of custard. The squashy clump in its sweet puddle may be delicious, but would you want to live in the landscape on your plate? Many people do, and my book is about the fantasies of runaways, beachcombers and children who refuse to grow up. Some islands, of course, are made of sterner, stonier stuff than eggs and sugar. Throughout history they have been the resorts of hermits, places where there was nothing to do but meditate on eternity. An island, whether actual or mental, offers artists the gift of detachment.

My own feelings are more ambivalent, because my island was assigned to me, not chosen like the retreats of the escapists and ascetics my book investigates. Not all islands are irresponsibly relaxing or erotically congenial, as daydreamers imagine. Islands can induce claustrophobia and panic: here you are confronted by edges, or by the end.

On maps, Tasmania – the island that supplied me with my skewed angle of vision – seems to be fraying. Like a body torn apart, the peninsulas south of Hobart trail off into arms, then tenuous fingers. Before long, the fragmentary limbs and digits crumble into a flailing ocean. Abrupt cliffs of cracked stone mark the point where land stops – almost where the earth stops, since further south there is only a continent of ice, now stealthily thawing. The west coast of my island is a cold, matted jungle with no shore, and on the east coast there are beaches where the mountains, reduced to bright white grains, sift away as if trickling through an hour glass.

Islands have outlines, which means that we are tempted to read them as bodies or at least as objects, a key to nature's intent in forming them. In *Treasure Island*, Jim Hawkins likens the island on the map to a fat dragon standing upright (though the diagram in Robert Louis Stevenson's book is amorphously blobby, like an ink blot in which you can see whatever you please). Those who ponder the map of Tasmania – as I did when I was growing up there, staring at its tapering, serrated shape as if I was already looking down from some cool vertical distance – mostly cast metaphorical aspersions on it. The nineteenth-century novelist Marcus Clarke, who wrote about the period when the island was a brutal prison camp for British felons, thought that it resembled a biscuit gnawed by rats. Off the coast, the protruding clumps called the Three Thumbs reminded him of 'melted lead spilt into water' – and who but a malformed, blundering giant would want three thumbs anyway? The hunt for analogies and explanations continues. Long after I left home my parents sent me a letter rack pieced together from shards of pine felled in the Huon Valley, with the name of the state burned into the pale wood. Attached to the side is a copper map of Tasmania, which when rendered in metal resembles a shield or a police badge, at once defensive and imposingly officious. The map, however, is fixed to a small apple carved out of darker wood, a reminder that, after the transportation of convicts ended, Tasmania recreated itself as a peaceable Eden, an orchard where apples were grown for export to England. The map looks eroded, abraded; with its round maternal curves, the apple tries to atone for that. But if rats nibble biscuits, it's worth remembering that worms can infiltrate apples. Didn't the acquisition of knowledge begin with the first bite of a forbidden fruit, and lead on to expulsion from the garden? I often look at the letter rack, which has never held any letters, and think about what its little symbols are whispering.

To be born in Tasmania, when it happened to me in 1948, was to be a castaway, set apart from a remote, unreachable world. Not wanting to accept that this was necessarily my lot in life, I toyed with other ways of explaining how I came to be there. The option of shipwreck had to be ruled out, though spars of rock jutted out of the stormy ocean beneath Tasmania, waiting to rip holes in passing boats. I was relieved when I learned that the stories about mariners thrown up on uncharted islands were actually parables – myths of nativity or of self-generation that apply to us all, whether or not we have suffered nautical mishaps. 'To be born,' J. M. Barrie helpfully explained, 'is to be wrecked on an island.' Islands are an existential terrain, and they prompt generalities like this. Matthew Arnold saw each of us as 'enislèd' in the sea of life. After reading *Robinson Crusoe*, Virginia Woolf concluded that 'All humanity is on a desert island alone'. An island convinced me of my disconnection – a quirk that I carried with me when I left Tasmania. Though I should not blame the place for my introversion, I have always felt beached inside my own body, marooned in my head. I refuse to believe John Donne's pious claim that no man is an island. As I see it, every man is one – by which I mean that I am. Islands break up a low-lying continental norm, and force you to recognize their singularity and your own. When W. H. Auden went to Iceland, he reported that 'This is an island and therefore/ Unreal'. Its geysers and whales and exotically vile food – including soup seasoned with brilliantine – gave him grounds for thinking so; he was born in the English Midlands, so of course he placed Iceland beyond the frontier of the familiar and filled it up with quaint absurdities. But his joke marked a failure of understanding: the experience should have persuaded him that all definitions of reality are relative. Crossing from Naples to Sicily in 1787, Goethe – born in landlocked Frankfurt – reflected on the novelty of seeing himself entirely surrounded by water. Until this happens, he said, you have no conception of the world or of your place in it. The boat he sailed on was his floating island, buffeted by bad weather – a speck of self, perilously exposed to the violent uncertainty of nature. Goethe's revelation was second nature to me, a geographical and psychological given. I thought of Tasmania as a raft adrift on turbulent water, with its whittled base pointing towards Antarctica.

I was vaguely aware of what my small, entrenched self had lost. My island, like the ego, was the product of an irreparable breach. The process of separation is usually violent – not the involuntary parting of clasped hands, but more like what employers who eject you from the premises call 'severance'. Tasmania, I discovered at school, had once been joined to the rest of the Australian continent by a land bridge, which capsized and left a flooded strait. I found the rupture easy to imagine: a sound like ripped cloth, the screams that accompany birth, a spillage of fluid. When you become conscious, you see that you have been set adrift, your lifeline cut. Or else the floor sinks beneath your feet, mocking the very idea of stability; you cling to a clump of soil and rock like a man who clutches a remnant of his shattered ship. If you think about them, islands induce a light-headed sense of vertigo. 'An island,' as the Portuguese novelist José Saramago once remarked, 'is the most fortuitous of events'. Its birth is an accident, perhaps a disaster: either it has fallen off the edge of a continent, or it is a sinking body with a head that battles to stay above the water. The group known as the Marianas, which contains Guam, manages to raise a few modest humps in the level Pacific. It is probably fortunate that the opaque ocean conceals the abyss beneath: these islands are the peaks of mountains seven miles high.

My island's secession from the mainland turned it into a place of solitary confinement. When in 1803 colonial administrators decided to establish a penal colony in Van Diemen's Land (the name given to it by its discoverer Abel Tasman, who made the governor of the Dutch East India Company its symbolic overlord), they hardly needed to invest in bars, cages and manacles. The angry seas and the dense bush further inland formed natural barriers, so that runaways either drowned or died of starvation in the narrow valleys. Most people think of islands as places to escape to: the image of a circular clump of land with a few palm trees and a slice of white sand is guaranteed to sell holidays. My island, however, was a place to escape from. I rehearsed my own departure in my first lamely literal flight of imagination, undertaken while still at school. It is only because the pages were thrown away long ago that I risk thinking about them: adolescent longing is so ferociously intense, and so pitifully helpless when it runs headlong into the obstacles of actuality.

I called my story *Escape from Killarni Island*, fancying that the name sounded tropical. I already knew how different islands were when you reached Polynesia, a name which – admitting European bemusement about the uncountable archipelagos strewn across the Pacific – simply means 'many islands'. My father, who had got as far as New Guinea during the war, used to refer to the region dismissively as 'the islands': places, in his view, of humid stupor and seething darkness, very different from his tame and temperate home. At the end of the war, when troop ships were in short supply, he spent a few bored months in New Guinea awaiting repatriation. Escape for him meant going back to where he came from, marrying, never leaving Tasmania again, and blaming those indiscriminate islands for any subsequent upsets to his bowels. A generation later, my urges were the opposite ones. I don't remember what the characters in my story were escaping from. Their parents, probably; from a life they had not chosen. The plot hardly mattered, because in most stories set on an island the urgent need is to get there so that the dreaming can begin. Sometimes the excuse is a search for treasure, though the island itself is usually the prize, the reward at the end of the quest. We happily accept whatever contrivance is required to deposit the characters on that unexplored beach. The rest is up to them, and all options are available: they can reconstruct civilization like Robinson Crusoe, or destroy it like the feral children in William Golding's *Lord of the Flies*. My plot made no sense, because it was dictated by my own contradictory impulses. Before my surrogates could escape from Killarni Island, they had to escape to it. Killarni was a place of naked liberty and unregulated pleasure, an alternative to the starchy stringencies of routine. Why then was there a need for a second escape? Where else was there to go, if not back to a home that was unhappy but at least familiar? Behind the sunny fictitious paradise lay the more shadowy island that was my reality.

The characters somehow had to be catapulted from Tasmania to the South Seas. Undeterred by the fact that I had never been in a plane, I imagined a journey by air. I huffed and puffed to get the plane into the sky, then – self-spiting as ever – pulled it back to earth by making it crash on Killarni. Inevitably I described the way Bass Strait looked from far above: the whole point of the effort was to get across that barrier, which divided me from the other worlds I wanted to experience. Projecting my own excitement onto the water, I described waves frothing and frisking. A well-travelled adult pointed out my mistake. Seen from a height, the sea is immobile, as though painted, so my waves would have to restrain themselves. I don't think any subsequent critical comment has ever depressed me as much as this did, because it revealed that imagination – at least in my case – could not overturn actuality; I was grounded all over again. A teacher contributed another criticism, changing a single word. The story contained a pair of malevolent grown-ups, whose conspiring was overheard by the children. I made one of these villains casually address the other as 'darling' – a word I had never heard anyone actually use, although it was bandied about by the glossy immaculate foreigners I saw in films, so I must have thought it appropriate for the small offshore world I was trying to picture. When my teacher returned the story, 'darling' had been crossed out with a red pen and replaced by the chaster 'dear' – appropriate for a church social, not for a muttered midnight conversation on a beach. This was my warning about the impropriety of fantasy, even grimmer than the earlier advice about optics. I never finished writing the story because I had no way of getting off the island, either mentally or physically. I abandoned the characters there, as if leaving them to perish.

A few years later I made my own escape, and got as far as England without misadventure. But Tasmania went with me: it remains my point of orientation, the spot I look for first on any map. Insularity defines who or what I am. When Darwin visited the Galápagos in 1835, he noticed that the giant tortoises on the various islands in the group had differently shaped shells. They wore a range of architectural models on their backs: domes in one place, arches in another. Not only were all of them different from anything that existed on the mainland, each insulated group (including the seven kinds of mocking-thrushes native to seven different islands in the group) might have been 'a different set of beings'. Islands narrow and concentrate the rules of selection, encouraging oddities; they are, although I did not realize it when I lived on one, breeding grounds for idiosyncrasy.

Everyone who was not allotted an island of their own at birth seems to have adopted or acquired one. The idea is portable, and can be enjoyed without leaving home or getting out of your car. In Michael Mann's film noir *Collateral* a harassed Los Angeles taxi driver pins up behind his rear-vision mirror a postcard of a tiny island in the Maldives, shaped like a fried egg. He glances at it whenever the passengers in the back seat are obnoxious or deranged; it serves as a pacifier, adjusting his pulse to the rhythm of waves flopping langorously on a beach, and allows him to go on a dozen vacations in a day. The image and the word that names it encapsulate a desperate dream. In Tennessee Williams's novel *The Roman Spring of Mrs Stone*, the heroine's husband has a heart attack on a flight from Rome to Athens. Distraught, she demands that the pilot land on an Aegean island – a green mound studded with cubes of white – that she sees far below. It is not possible, she is told; the plane carries its dead passenger on through 'the brilliantly vacuous air'. Mrs Stone beats on the thickened, impervious window and shrieks '*Island! Island!*' The reiterated word is eloquent, like an imploded aria. An island means grounding, stability, though Mrs Stone might not want to admit that it could also be a burial place; as it smoothly recedes, gliding into the past, it comes to stand for a happiness that is irrecoverably lost – time made visible in space. Our fears and desires can both find a habitat on such innocuous, anonymous specks.

I pointed myself towards continents and cities, mistakenly convinced that the world had a centre that was situated somewhere far to the north. But those who began in or near that imaginary centre have always moved in the opposite direction, curious about the outer edges of possibility where cities run out and continents crumble into islands. In 1814 Keats began his poetic career with a homage to his adored predecessor Edmund Spenser. The opening of his poem summarizes the agenda of poetry itself:

> Ah! could I tell the wonders of an isle
> That in the fairest lake had placèd been, ...
> For sure so fair a place was never seen,
> Of all that ever charmed romantic eye.

Keats never saw such an island, because he did his travelling inside the books he read. During the 1870s Arthur Rimbaud escaped from France to a succession of islands that offered him the chance to enjoy alternative lives. In Java he served as a soldier in the Dutch colonial army, in Cyprus he worked in a quarry. He described his restlessness when he boasted

> I have seen sidereal archipelagos! and islands
> Whose delirious skies are open to the sea-wanderer.

Rimbaud's archipelagos no longer float on the sea; projected into the sky, they turn into galaxies that beckon the entranced, uprooted poet. A more private island can represent the sanctuary of the self, the hushed source of creativity. In 1890 W. B. Yeats volunteered for a life of retirement on a lake isle like the one Keats imagined, set in Lough Gill, County Sligo:

> I will arise and go now, and go to Innisfree,
> And a small cabin build there, of clay and wattle made:
> Nine bean-rows will I have there, a hive for the honey-bee,
> And live alone in the bee-loud glade.

What Yeats craves, as he says, is peace, purple noons, evenings filled with linnets' wings, and 'lake water lapping': the ocean bottled. The cultivation of that kitchen garden is merely an alibi. The cabin is a studio; the hermit's occupation is writing poems.

During the 1940s the novelist Marguerite Yourcenar moved to Mount Desert Island off the coast of Maine, where she felt she could live at a tangent to the obnoxious United States. A French sailor named the place during the seventeenth century, alluding to its stark, treeless peak; Yourcenar described it as a Corsica that had somehow strayed north. She came to think of it as her sovereign domain, and soon made a metaphor of it. In 1956 she explained to a French friend that America was harsh and economically brutish, except for 'small islands of public-spiritedness'. The image is paradoxical, even hypocritical: islands are aesthetic refuges from the confused, congested public realm, so it is odd to see them enlisted as models of civic virtue. Milan Kundera's use of the conceit is more logical, perhaps because he has no actual island in view. Kundera claims that the deafness of the elderly Beethoven was a boon because it removed him from the distractions of society and made possible his late music, which is 'a miracle, an island'. In phrases that might be musical variations, Kundera beautifully equates the two words.

Placed outside average human experience, islands are other or nether worlds. In 1890 Chekhov left Moscow and travelled 6,500 miles across Siberia by horse, ferry, riverboat and train to the prison island of Sakhalin. When he arrived, he felt he had reached 'the end of the world', or at least the beginning of unknowable Asia. He pointed out that Sakhalin was 'twice as large as Greece, and one and a half times the size of Denmark', but islands are defined by isolation not by bulk. The convicts on Sakhalin could glimpse freedom on a hazy shore just across the water; though the mainland remained out of reach, they were sustained – Chekhov reported – by their fanatical belief in the possibility of escape, which for them was a 'return from the dead'. 'Why have I come here?' he asked in *The Island*, his account of the futile, altruistic expedition. He found Sakhalin to be literally indescribable: he could not tell stories about a society that trapped both prisoners and jailers in a cycle of maddeningly repetitive tedium. He felt that he had visited the underworld, and consorted with a population of shackled, shuffling ghosts. On the way back to Moscow he made a detour to Hong Kong and Singapore, and reported that 'I have been in hell, which is Sakhalin, and in paradise, which is Ceylon'. His expedition took him from a frigid inferno to a tropical heaven whose delights were sensual not spiritual, and both extremities were situated on islands.

Between those subhuman and superhuman poles, our history can be read as a long, digressive journey around a world that has fragmented into islands. Man the traveller, explorer and fantasist has better luck on the water than if he trudges overland. The journey is chancier, because tides and storms can revise his itinerary, but the islands encountered along the way are unmapped exceptions to the norm. Homer's Odysseus spends ten years on the return journey to Ithaca after the Trojan war; the islands he visits while meandering across the Mediterranean are optional worlds, like extraneous planets that have splashed down into the sea. Unreconciled to gravity, Aeolia hovers in mid-air, held aloft by the breath of Aeolus, god of the four winds. On one island, Circe works her deforming magic; another is the lair of the Cyclops; on a third, the sun puts its oxen out to pasture. Odysseus samples them all, then sails away towards his own island (which is actually more like a peninsula, still vestigially linked to the reality of the mainland). Can we believe that he stayed there? In *The Divine Comedy*, Dante encounters a speaking tongue of flame in hell, and learns that this fiery portent was once Ulysses. The hero confesses that he did not remain in Ithaca, but soon set off in search of other islands in the unpeopled region beyond the setting sun. On this last voyage, he travels west through the Pillars of Hercules, the two mountains flanking the Straits of Gibraltar that set the limits of the classical world. He advances into the ocean and sails on for five months, veering towards the southern terminus of the earth. There a mountainous island rears up before him. He has reached the site of paradise, which, after Christ harrowed hell, became the location of purgatory. Dante's sacred geography identified that sudden pinnacle as the only land in the southern hemisphere: when Satan was hurled out of heaven he supposedly dropped into these seas, so the other continents hastily migrated north of the equator to avoid contagion. Like Tasmania, the island is cast away in uncharted water; at least Dante gives it a spiritual pedigree. Ulysses wonders at its daunting heights, and his crew rejoices at the prospect of landfall. Then a violent storm rebuffs them: as pagan unbelievers, they have no right to enter this posthumous realm. Their ship founders, and they all drown.

The world sealed and fortified by the Pillars of Hercules opened outwards in the sixteenth century, when Spanish, Portuguese and English explorers annexed new lands that oozed wealth: precious metals, or exotic commodities like tobacco and potatoes. Now islands were synonymous with condiments, titillating luxuries. The Moluccas in eastern Indonesia were nicknamed the Spice Islands because they were the source of cloves, black pepper and nutmeg, brought to Europe by Venetian traders and later by the merchants of the Dutch East India Company. Competing empires squabbled over the spoils of these remote places. The imagination, standing back from the adventure of invasion and exploitation, valued islands as unorthodox microcosms, ersatz works of art. Prospero in *The Tempest* is wrecked on a barren isle which he enriches with his magical powers. Banquets materialize in mid-air, classical goddesses swoop down on visits, and below the waterline sightless eyes harden into vitreous pearls. The English emigrants in Andrew Marvell's poem 'Bermudas' rejoice in their discovery of an island balmier and lusher than their own. The grass is enamelled, pomegranates glow in the fragrant air, and figs beg to be eaten. Marvell's settlers luxuriate in this tropical idyll, though their puritanism supplies their idle, hedonistic life with a moral justification: they are the elect, and in their song they smugly thank God for treating them to a foretaste of heaven.

Late in the eighteenth century, exploration extended to the South Seas, where different kinds of islands shimmered in the soupy, sweltering air. In the Pacific, there was no continent for such islands to secede from; they rose directly from the ocean floor, discharging lethal heat. Byron morosely likened himself to one of those blackened chimneys that poke through the water:

> The fire that on my bosom preys
> Is lone as some volcanic isle;
> No torch is kindled at its blaze –
> A funeral pile.

Emotions were Byron's internal river of lava, leaving poems behind as their residue when the scorching emission cooled. In his voluntary exile, he wrote letters to his trapped compatriots in which he sneered at Britain as 'your foggy Island': it was the wrong kind of island for him, occupied by a sniffy middle class, made damp and dreary by weather unconducive to sensual pleasure. At the fountain of Arethusa in Ithaca, he remembered Prospero's renunciation of magical power at the end of *The Tempest*. 'If this isle were mine,' he told his friend Trelawny, 'I would break my staff and bury my book.' But Prospero does not contemplate permanent residence, and in returning home cedes ownership to Caliban, the native master of the place. To forswear the commanding staff and bury the book of spells meant, for Byron, to abandon poetry. If the isle was his, why should he bother devising fantastical islands? Islands like those he described stood for the stubbornly autonomous mind, combining proud self-creation and violent self-destruction. Exiled on St Helena in the South Atlantic, Napoleon spent the last years of his life walking round in circles on his open prison. To amuse himself he played cards, cultivated a vegetable patch, and read novels. The books were a better consolation than games of chance or crops of potatoes: they persuaded him, as he told his companion the Comte de Las Cases, that 'Imagination rules the world!' Better an imaginary island than an actual empire? The poet and military adventurer Gabriele d'Annunzio invoked the same image after the collapse of his nationalist regime at Fiume on the Adriatic coast. In 1922 he wrote to Mussolini announcing his scornful resignation from politics: '"Make of yourself an island", says a sage of Asia. That is what I have done for myself.'

Like all romantic dreams, this solipsistic fantasy was available for purchase by those with limited imaginations and limitless funds. King Ludwig II of Bavaria chose an island in the lake of Chiemsee as the location for one of his palaces, a sumptuously empty asylum. After the American civil war, tycoons built pseudo-feudal residences on the Thousand Islands in the St Lawrence River, like medieval barons holed up in their moated castles; one island in the group was acquired by the Yale Skull and Bones secret society, which presumably needed a secluded setting to practise its piratical rituals. Recluses like Howard Hughes and the deposed Shah of Iran sheltered on Paradise Island in the Bahamas. This swampy wilderness was once known as Hog Island, though its name was spiritualized in deference to the millionaires who took up residence there. Aristotle Onassis established a plutocratic court on the Ionian island of Skorpios, while his fellow magnate Stavros Niarchos treated himself to Spetsopoula in the Aegean. At the end of his life, Rudolf Nureyev bought a miniature archipelago off Positano. He saw it as his 'magic abode', like Prospero's island, and prostituted himself to pay for it: 'I've got to be able to finance my island,' he said when explaining why he signed demeaning contracts for provincial tours. As his Aids symptoms worsened, he worried about how much longer he had left, and – still waiting for the tumbledown huts on Li Galli to be made habitable – he plaintively told his current lover 'I want my island to be finished'. After filming *Mutiny on the Bounty* in French Polynesia, Marlon Brando pocketed the atoll of Tetiaroa near Tahiti, where he dozed on the beach and mimicked the gait of the hermit crabs. Fletcher Christian and the *Bounty* mutineers had set up an outlaw commune on Pitcairn Island; Brando wanted to follow their example, and thought of Tetiaroa as his 'Zen heaven' – at least until his son, prophetically named Christian, killed one of the natives. Now a film star's portfolio is incomplete unless it contains such a trophy. Mel Gibson has bought the title to a few bits of rock in the Pacific, and Leonardo DiCaprio owns Blackadore Caye off Belize, which he wants to turn into a resort for tourists with an ecological conscience.

At their most crazily imperious, the rich invent islands, doing God's work all over again. Fisher Island, south of Miami Beach, is a sliver of land dredged from the sea in 1905. It can be approached only by yacht, helicopter, or a ferry which will not accept you as a passenger unless you produce an invitation from one of the five hundred residents. The islanders have their own cashless economy, with membership cards to tot up digital debts. Caged toucans and macaws – let out once a day for a stroll with a professional bird walker – supply a soundtrack of jungle muzak, even though the undergrowth has been flattened to install tennis courts and golf courses. During the 1970s the Las Vegas real-estate developer Michael Oliver constructed an unreal estate for himself in the Pacific. Oliver built up the micronation of Minerva, as he called it, from reclaimed land. Extra loads of sand freighted in from Australia raised the height of the reef and allowed a flagpole to be erected. The proprietor enthroned a puppet president, put his own currency into circulation, and announced plans for the establishment of a libertarian Utopia. The experiment was curtailed when troops from Tonga annexed the place. At the time, it seemed an absurd folly; now, however, developers are busy manufacturing islands. In Dubai a resort called The World fragments the five continents into leasable islands, which loll on the torpid waters of the Persian Gulf like interlinked life-rafts. European countries or American states have been reduced to individual lots, and residents can be the sole inhabitants of their own exclusive Switzerland or Kansas. There is no need to worry about porous borders, because cartographic lines have been replaced by canals which ensure that the provinces remain apart. When the project is complete, the artificial settlements will add up into a map of the globe, although the pattern will only be visible from high above. The aerial perspective is telling. For the rich, islands like these are half-way houses, a stage in their flight from an earth on which the rest of us are condemned to continue living.

Homer's gods warn Odysseus against trespassing on the island where Helios pastures his oxen, which are sacred to the sun. Our universe has outgrown such embargoes, and science explores islands in the sky that once were inaccessible or fatal to men. NASA recently sent a spacecraft called *Ulysses* to orbit the sun's polar caps and track sunspots; no offended deity interfered with its mission. Following the example of Aeolia, islands have migrated to outer space, taking castaways like Prospero or Robinson Crusoe with them. During the 1950s the science fiction film *Forbidden Planet* reinvented Shakespeare's wizard as a nuclear physicist stationed in a remote galaxy, and in 1964 Defoe's sailor joined him in orbit in Byron Haskin's film *Robinson Crusoe on Mars*. Haskin's version of the red planet lay near to hand: the film was made in Death Valley, over the mountains behind Los Angeles. More recently, islands have retreated into cyberspace, which is both further away and nearer than Mars. In the virtual world of Second Life, you can buy a variety of 'islands' that serve as resorts where like-minded friends can network or sell merchandise. A getaway measuring sixteen acres costs two thousand dollars, with an additional monthly fee for maintaining the non-existent terrain. Although these islands have a merely notional existence, four different physical types are illustrated on the website. They resemble bits of a mutilated body, like severed ears or internal organs afloat on the water. But reconnection to the organism is possible, and if you buy more islands you can slot these particles into each other to make a so-called 'continent'. As in so many stories about islands, the ego stands on guard against intruders: Second Lifers are assured that they can 'limit access' to their island.

'Maybe,' suggest the organizers of the scheme, 'you have visions of a world under your control' – which has always been the islander's crazily idealistic dream. The sidereal archipelagos glimpsed by Rimbaud are no longer a metaphor, and not so deliriously remote. The possibility makes me regret rejecting the island where my own memories are interred; too late, I begin to see the uses of a second life.

2. FIRST AND LAST THINGS

Everything began, perhaps, on an island. It's just as possible that everything could end there.

My island, like Sakhalin, was at one of the world's vanishing points: convicts transported to Van Diemen's Land were effectively obliterated, or excreted. But myth has the power to award centrality to an island, rather than relegating it to the outskirts of creation. Islands can be umbilical: Homer describes the abode of the nymph Calypso as the navel of the ocean. It is the nutritious bud from which all else grows, and Calypso, like a mother reluctant to cut the cord, detains Odysseus there for seven years. Is her island a uterine shelter, where we can curl up and postpone the struggles that begin when we are expelled into reality? The anatomical hint shocked William Cowper, who in 1791 in his poetic translation of *The Odyssey* covered up the navel by calling Calypso's island 'the central boss/ Of the ocean'. He did not mean that she bossily managed the waves: a boss is an ornamental knob, placed at the point where the thrusting forces converge in an arch. Buildings, for Cowper, were more respectable than bodies. His bowdlerized island may no longer be a nourishing source but it is still a presiding nub, decorated to enhance its significance. Geographers have sometimes followed the promptings of myth. The two hundred islands scattered in the Aegean were called the Cyclades because they encircled Delos, which floated above the water until Zeus chose it to shelter his lover Leto, and Poseidon, to mark this divine favour, attached it to our secular globe. Inside this protective circle, Delos was sanctified. An early account of Japan's origins relates a similar fable. The gods peered down from the bridge of heaven, curious about what might be hiding in the wet murk below. They poked a jewelled spear into the void, and made contact with the ocean. Flecks of brine clung to the tip of the spear; dripping off, the salty residue congealed into an island. The gods called it Ono-goro-jima, and decided that it would be the pillar that supports the world. If only someone had told me such a story about Tasmania!

While the Japanese gods began with one small, precious island, the God of Genesis created the whole world at once. A divine edict separated land from water, which is a recipe for forming continents. Islands, the result of fragmentation, had no proper place in the original scheme: reason enough, you might think, for atheism. In the middle of the eighteenth century, the Swedish botanist Linnaeus questioned the official story, and isolated a primal island from the continuous landmass that Genesis expects us to imagine. What puzzled the tidy taxonomic mind of Linnaeus was the discrepancy between the earth's far-flung, divergent species and the claim in Genesis that they all cohabited in Eden or in Noah's ark. He decided that the true story of creation was not the account of that first busy week but the tale of the flood. As the waters receded, the ark ran aground on Ararat, conventionally identified as a mountain in modern-day Turkey; it was from here that the disembarking flocks and herds rayed out to increase and multiply. Could it be that Ararat was an island not a mountain peak (which is what many islands, looked at from beneath, actually are)? And could that island – which presumably had a steep, graduated terrain to accommodate different creatures that belong in tropical, temperate and polar climates – be the true Eden? Linnaeus proposed that we forget about continents, which only emerged later as the drainage continued. 'One small island only,' he said, 'was in the beginning raised above the surface of the waters.'

The scene is appealingly primordial: picture a head emerging from the waves, separating itself from a fluid, undifferentiated life as it seeks a landfall. But if you look at it another way, islands are dead ends, cemeteries. Volcanic islands take shape when the eruptive fire cools into a scab of ash and scorched rock. Off the southern coast of Iceland, an eruption that began in 1963 and lasted for almost four years belched up Surtsey, named after Surtur, the Norse god of fire. No sooner had the island been created than the grinding process of destruction got underway; flayed by wind, nibbled by water, Surtsey is now less than half its original size. The coral islands of the Indian Ocean, as Darwin discovered during his voyage on *The Beagle* in the 1840s, were compiled by corpses. An epochal collapse dragged rocky islands into the sea, while the coral fringing them pushed up to form a barrier. An atoll was for Darwin the grave of an islet, and reefs – whitening as they age, like human beings – were armies of skeletal insects, fused in death. When men reversed the action of the gods and tested their own capacity to destroy the world, they did so on a coral island like those Darwin visited. Between 1946 and 1958 the United States detonated twenty-three nuclear weapons on Bikini Atoll in the Marshall Islands. Even before the tests, Bikini had been set aside as a mortuary. Ships sunk during the war in the Pacific were dumped inside the reef, and the island's homepage still appeals for divers to fish salvage from the rusted hulks. The two hundred human inhabitants were evacuated before the first explosion, but kept under observation as case studies of radioactive contamination. The blast atomized an array of battleships in the lagoon, with a captive crew of pigs, goats and rats on board. Islands much smaller than mine were the laboratory in which the apocalypse was rehearsed.

Insularity teaches you to be paranoid: Tasmania, although it was no kind of geopolitical prize, seemed during my Cold War childhood to be the ultimate target. I blame my gloom on Nevil Shute's *On the Beach*, which shadowed my adolescence like a dense, suffocating cloud. In the novel, a trivial, unintelligible war in the northern hemisphere has ended in an atomic explosion. Humankind is killed off by radiation sickness, which drifts south across the equator and filters down to the lowliest latitudes until Shute's characters, just across Bass Strait in Melbourne, are the last huddled survivors – except, of course, for those confined to Tasmania, who are expected to last a few weeks longer. I suppose I should have derived a meagre comfort from that short postponement. Instead what I remember noticing, with a flush of shame and indignation, was that the bonus made no difference to Shute's mainland-ers. None of them considered moving interstate, as we called it; to die on the continent was better than living for an extra month on our island. Yet when I imagined an epilogue to Shute's plot, I wondered what difference the extermi-nation might actually make. The sullen mountains that surveyed our house would still be there, although there would be no need for the house or for all the others like it, assembled as rapidly as cardboard cartons and easily disas-sembled; the beaches at the margins of the lapsing land would be unaltered, except for the absence of picnickers and broiling sunbathers. Perhaps islands are meant to be deserted.

Wrong as it is, I now think of Tasmania as a burial site. The aboriginal inhabitants compliantly died off, at least according to the official history, to make way for colonial usurpers. The penitentiary at Port Arthur has an Isle of the Dead, a mound of scrub in the bay put to use as a cemetery in 1833. Death here was not a democratic equalizer: convicts were shovelled into mass graves, while free settlers occupied private plots and were honoured with headstones and flattering testimonials. But they all made the short journey across the water, which formalized their removal from the land of the living.

Thinking about what once was home, I seem to be standing on that small, morbid island. Every time I receive a letter from Tasmania, I know before opening it that there has been a death in my extended family. My relatives do not keep me informed about births, which are also happening: that, as they rightly feel, is no concern of mine. I too, having disappeared elsewhere, am as good as dead.

A man in naval uniform, with a stiff-brimmed cap and an officious braided epaulette, slouches against a palm tree. His posture is unmilitary, and he strums a guitar while he croons about sailing to paradise. Every so often he arrives at a refrain and smoochily descends to a huskier, more suggestive vocal register. The repeated line is 'On an island with you', and it works like a bait cast on the air. Hearing it, a mermaid swims through stagnating water with the velocity of a torpedo and strides ashore. Dressed in a sarong, with a magnolia in her greased, imperturbably coiffed hair, she sashays towards the singing sailor and stops his mouth with a kiss. He accepts the compliment, and overlooks the fact that she has dripped all over his pristine, pleated white uniform. She is Esther Williams, he is Ricardo Montalban, and this is the opening of the MGM musical *On an Island with You*, made in 1948. Although Montalban's voice is tuneless, the line he so insistently repeats has an axiomatic appeal. To invoke an island is a guaranteed aid to seduction.

The goddess of love had an island as her birthplace: a temple honouring Aphrodite was found on Cythera in the Aegean Sea, and in tales about the Olympian deities she spirits her favourites there for sessions of uninterrupted enjoyment. The terrain of Cythera is bare, eroded, riven by earthquakes. We prefer to imagine it as Watteau did in his *Pèlerinage à l'île de Cythère*, painted in 1717 and now in the Louvre. The goddess was born, according to the myth, from the spermatic foam of the waves, which is why she rides on a shell in Botticelli's depiction of the nativity of Venus. For Watteau, she is a

creature of the other elements – of fertile earth and breathy air, a personification of the fire that ignites desire. The hump of softly vegetated ground on
which the lovers linger could be the mound of Venus, and the billowy foliage
above is a discreet screen, like the canopy of a bed. The very air seems damp
with incense, permeated by colour that bleeds from the setting sun and is
exhaled by the palpitating breezes; the sultry atmosphere materializes in the
bodies of flying putti, which entwine into wreaths as if they too, despite their
chubby infancy, are anxious to couple. A dog's upright tail signals an excitement that is not suppressed by clothes or by timid moral precepts.

But are these people travelling to Cythera or regretfully quitting it?
They carry the kind of staff on which pilgrims lean during their long, painful
journeys of expiation, although rather than visiting a Christian shrine they
have left flowers at the statue of a pagan goddess. On a slope near the waiting
boat, they cast sad, satiated glances backwards at a pleasure that already lies
in the past. Perhaps they are leaving because the island's delights have been
chastened: the flesh of Venus has been changed to unfeeling stone, her lower,
libidinous parts replaced by a stark geometrical column. When Watteau
repainted the scene later – this version is now in the Charlottenburg Palace in
Berlin – he gave Venus back the rest of her plump, spongy body, allowed her
to frolic with Cupid on her pedestal, and even let one of the impudent putti
clamber onto the plinth as an intermediary between the warmth of human
ardour and the frigid stasis of art. At the same time he inserted a new allegorical admonition, a warning that this is a place we can only visit, and from
which we must depart. Trophies of other, nobler human endeavours – a lyre
and a suit of armour – lie at the base of the monument, sacrificed to the pursuit
of love. The cheeky putto has stolen a conqueror's laurel crown and placed it at
the feet of Venus, who is free to trample her sterner rival, Mars. But how honest
is the renunciation? In the Berlin version, the winged putti cluster in rowdy
gangs above the anchored boat; they slither up its mast and tweak its flushed

sails, preparing to discharge their quivers of stimulating arrows. Like procurers, they coax the evacuees to board the golden vessel, which is a sea-going bed. The lovers are taking the island home with them, and the boat will serve as their rhythmically undulating mattress.

Explorers often fancied that they had rediscovered the lair of Venus. Arriving in Tahiti in 1768, Bougainville named the island Nouvelle Cythère. It was a paradise, he thought, of innocent, frolicsome nudity (into which European visitors soon brought venereal disease). Darwin too, watching from *The Beagle* as Tahiti swam into view, called it 'a new Cythera' or 'the Queen of the Islands'. In his *Journal of Researches* he relied on a more politely evasive allusion to the myth, saying only that Tahiti 'must forever remain classical to the voyager in the South Seas'. A merry crowd gathered on Point Venus to greet the ship; the goddess, however, had been deposed, and when Darwin's party landed, they were taken straight to the house of the district's missionary. Debussy had better luck in a less exotic location during the summer of 1904, which he spent on Jersey with Emma Bardac, the mistress for whose sake he deserted his wife. While there he composed *L'Isle joyeuse*, in which the piano pays tribute to Watteau's painting. The pianist's fluttery, frisking hands brush away the melancholy suspension of Watteau's Cythera. The pictorial island exists in space, and the people on it, whether coming or going, are immobilized like Venus on her pedestal. Debussy's musical island belongs in time, which hectically hurtles towards the climax that Watteau postpones. After eight minutes of frenzied play, *L'Isle joyeuse* ends in a spasm of abandonment that is abruptly, almost prematurely, curtailed. You are free to be graphic or even pornographic about what happens on Cythera so long as the scenery remains invisible. ·

The myth, as inextinguishable as sex itself, has a contemporary progeny. One of the most energetic of today's porn stars – actually born in the Mormon stronghold of Salt Lake City, although she moved to Las Vegas to get her career started – goes by the startlingly classical name of Cytherea. She occupies a pink site insulated in the wilds of cyberspace; here she can be found demonstrating her special skill, which is 'squirting' or female ejaculation. Though she may live in a desert or in the impalpable ether, she produces her own frothy sea of fluid to encircle her imaginary island.

All islands can be divided between a pair of gods, competitive but complementary: Eros and Thanatos. Eros governs male desire; in league with Aphrodite, who sponsors female yearnings, he is responsible for the notion that islands are aphrodisiac places. Thanatos – born of the union between Night and Darkness, and twinned with Hypnos, the spirit of sleep – is more obscure, as befits his parentage. He presides over our dying, and he, too, has his base on an island. It would be convenient if the place where we enjoy the companionable warmth of sex and that where we suffer a chilly death could be set far apart, respectively in the balmy south and the cold north. The trouble is that they are neighbours.

In an allegorical reverie, Edgar Allan Poe imagines a schizoid island that exhibits both identities. At its western end, it has a 'radiant harem of garden beauties', with vegetation that blushes and glows, and trees as lithe as young bodies. In the east, cypresses cast doomy shadows, hillocks like graves are overrun by rosemary and rue, and an 'ebony flood' erodes the shore. Poe's Island of the Fay, as he called it, is our world, alternating between summery glut and the misery of winter, or between fertility and extinction. In 1844 the poet Gérard de Nerval described a visit to Cythera, which turned out to be less erotically enticing than he expected. The memory that stayed with Nerval was of a hanged man mouldering on the gallows. To his friend Baudelaire, the sight enforced the coupling of sex and death. In his own poem about a voyage to Cythera, Baudelaire sees the island as a tarnished El Dorado, peopled by superannuated dandies. He expects a landscape of soft green myrtles; instead he sees Nerval's pole with its cross-bar, which he likens to a funereal cypress. Birds are attacking the corpse, pecking at its eyes and shredding its genitals with their beaks. Here is a true native of Cythera: a man whose joy is transformed into anguish, whose desires become posthumous torments. The poem concludes with a grim phallic joke. On her island, Baudelaire tells Venus, the only upright thing he sees is that gibbet. Its erection is not a conduit for gushing, burgeoning life but an apparatus of death.

Every castaway knows that a source of fresh water has to be located at once; without this, the island is a potentially lethal place. But why should we reverse the analogy by picturing death itself as an island? Arnold Böcklin's painting *Die Toteninsel* makes the connection seem logical and even reassuring, which is one reason why he produced so many copies: the first version was painted in 1880, then repeated with slight variations in 1883, 1884 and 1886. Böcklin shows an unknown traveller being calmly ferried across black water, conveyed between two worlds. On a clump of rock stands a mausoleum surrounded by cypresses. The boulders by the water are rough and shaggy, but the angular classical architecture behind them completes a transition from nature to art, which may be the same progress that implacably ushers us into posterity. While the rocks have mineral tints that are the colour of dried blood, the buildings look bleached, purged: according to the painting, the next world will be white, silent and severely rectilinear. Although Böcklin was trying to look beyond life, he drew on the scenery of an actual place in the Tyrrhenian Sea, off Naples. His model was the volcanic island of Ponza, which opens out in a sheer smooth welcoming crescent. Ponza is a wonderland of geological metaphors, with rocks that assumed teasingly human shapes when the lava solidified. One of them is said to resemble a monk; perhaps Böcklin remembered this when he painted the mummified guide standing in the boat – a psychopomp, the conductor who accompanies the soul on its the passage between time and eternity.

Emily Dickinson imagined a time when she would be 'An Island in dishonored Grass – /Whom none but Beetles – know.' The expected ocean around her grave – the circumambient sea, Jung's womb in which floating islands are buoyed up and nourished by the maternal element – is parched, changed to grass, which is what flesh will be turned into as the beetles work on it. Dickinson futilely manoeuvres to avoid that fate by displacing an adjective: it's not the grass that is dishonoured but the woman buried underneath, deflowered in her bed by worms. Böcklin's preview of what follows death is sterner but more heartening. The shrouded psychopomp will deposit the coffin in a vacant niche somewhere inside that white mausoleum, where the dead harden into marmoreal statues. The slim columnar cypresses could be an honour guard of sentinels.

Böcklin had been asked by a widow to supply a painting on the subject of bereavement. Its sedative calm was meant to be consoling, which is why he referred to it as the picture of 'a still place'. Among the other provisional descriptions he toyed with was 'an island graveyard'; his dealer Fritz Gurlitt – in an associative leap that made the island a symbol of death, not just a site of peaceful rest for the dead – gave the painting the title by which we now know it. Gurlitt's compound word *Toteninsel* fuses two ideas without explaining the affinity between them. Perhaps we accept the connection because we think of insulation as a sanitary precaution: an island quarantines the dead, since ghosts are supposedly unable to ford water. The superstition is so common that it has been written into public policy. In New York City, those who die penniless or unknown or unclaimed by loved ones are buried in gaping trenches on a scrappy stretch of land off the Bronx called Hart Island, which over the years has also served as a disposal area for delinquent children and for sailors from German U-boats caught snooping off the coast. Inmates from the penitentiary on Riker's Island are ferried in to bury the anonymous pine crates, then returned to their own morose outpost. Like the razor-wired fence that surrounds the potter's field on Hart Island, water cordons off spectres, reprobates and aliens.

In 1888, after copying *Die Toteninsel*, Böcklin painted a refutation of it in *Die Lebensinsel*. His island of life is a more tropical version of Watteau's Cythera, with limber-trunked palm trees writhing above the revels of classical nymphs and satyrs. Pairs of lovers, accompanied by cruising swans, wade in the shallow water around the raised green platform. Their immersion is a reminder that life, being about continuity, is best represented as a fluid state. Despite the copulatory frolics of *Die Lebensinsel*, Böcklin knew that islands are not convivial places. Even if you have a companion, how long will it be before you fret to escape from that intimacy? In 1882 he painted a commentary on the first and most delightfully insidious of Homer's islands, where Calypso traps Odysseus. The place consists of a cantilevered rock, on which nothing grows. Calypso, having draped a red cloth on the boulder, pines outside the cave that is her bedroom. Over her shoulder, she looks at a lover who has withdrawn to the furthest edge of their cramped domain. Odysseus ignores her and stares at the sea. His figure duplicates that of the psychopomp in *Die Toteninsel*: he has the same self-contained silhouette, hands clenched before him to signal disengagement, although his head is more pensively bowed and he lurks in shadow, like a negative or negation of the white guide in the boat. On an island of love, Böcklin's Odysseus is brooding about death, which might be preferable to this cloying idyll.

Alive, we are joined to others, like the couples in *Die Lebensinsel*. Death enforces our insularity because it is an experience that cannot be shared. In Cowper's poem 'The Castaway', written in 1799, a man swept overboard in a storm laments the fate of his drowned shipmates. 'We perished,' he reports as if posthumously, 'each alone'. In fact they perished together as a result of the same shipwreck, but death ignores that commonality. It requires them to form a single line; dying is the consequence and the consummation of individuality.

Earlier Cowper, himself painfully isolated by mental illness, had written some verses imagining the predicament of Alexander Selkirk, whose four years marooned on San Juan Fernández off the coast of Chile were the source for *Robinson Crusoe*. Cowper's Selkirk boasts that he is 'monarch of all I survey', that he lords it over 'the fowl and the brute'; the man in 'The Castaway' has no grounds for such swaggering confidence. Barrie likened birth to being wrecked on an island. The same could be said of death, although it is hardly necessary to contrive a wreck: the latterday island is our unavoidable destination.

Crusoe morosely remarks that his island condemns him to 'the silent life'. In the 'still place' painted by Böcklin, that silence is a stifling hush that forbids you to draw breath and go on living. Music, which moves in time, is mercifully able to break the spell. Rachmaninov and Max Reger composed symphonic tributes to *Die Toteninsel* in 1907 and 1913, completing the story. Böcklin's waves – confirming my mistake about Bass Strait – are fixed by paint as if by rigor mortis. Rachmaninov gives them back their swelling, slapping rhythm, and like funeral bells they wordlessly spell out the motto of a 'Dies Irae'. Does a day of judgment lie ahead, even though Böcklin's island is classical not Christian? Reger restores motion and animation with a series of muffled drum beats, like the thudding of a heart as it slows down to a halt. For Rachmaninov, the passage across the water is complicated by chromatic whirlpools. There are intervals of aching regret and moments of terrified expectancy: the occupant of Böcklin's coffin is brought back to life in order to die all over again, fearfully not serenely. Reger adds some stabbing outbursts of pain, inconceivable in the anaesthetized painting. A last metallic explosion suggests that death occurs only when the island is reached; after that there is peace, before a final jubilant announcement by the cymbals – salvation? At the end of Rachmaninov's symphonic poem, a riot of brass resounds from all corners of the sky, opening a crevasse into which the hapless soul tumbles while shuddering strings continue to mutter the 'Dies Irae'.

Both composers assume that Böcklin's island is a stage in a metaphysical journey. There is another possibility – truer perhaps to the mortified quiet of the painting, and to the inescapability of islands. The horror film *Isle of the Dead*, directed by Mark Robson in 1945, has its own solution to the mystery of the image. A woman in a cataleptic trance is sealed in a crate labelled 'Antiquitäten' and deposited in a tomb on a Greek island. She resurrects herself and goes on a killing spree: impaling victims on a trident, she is a vampire who seeks to 'drain all the life and joy from those who want to live'. The boat that transports the coffin in Böcklin's painting should have taken the young lovers off the island, but it is destroyed by Boris Karloff, who plays a dictatorial Greek general. He has a good reason for doing so, because there is plague on the mainland, but he may be imposing another embargo: like the woman buried alive, images – painted figures, or the ghosts that flicker on film – are undead things, and they belong on an island at a distance from the real, normal world. The spell of the painting suggests that art is a kind of death.

Virginia Woolf's *To the Lighthouse* ponders a journey to an island that is postponed at the start of the novel, but accomplished at the end in a morbidly triumphant ceremony. The pretext is to deliver supplies to the lighthouse keeper, who is stranded for a month at a time on a rock no bigger than a tennis lawn. The holiday home from which the Ramsays set out is on the Isle of Skye, though the location may be the result of some evasive verbal sidestepping in Woolf's mind. Ramsay is a Scots name, and Rasay is the island next to Skye, although the novelist's own family holidays were spent in the Isles of Scilly. But the details of topography matter less than the onerous import of the lonely, lucid tower, which can be approached only by those who are prepared to detach themselves from life and become artists – which for Woolf means turning yourself into a disembodied mind. The philosopher Mr Ramsay, who leads the expedition, prepares for it by repeating the motto of Cowper's Selkirk: we perish, each alone – but, as he might have added, the mind continues its speculative travelling after it has quit the grounded, gregarious body. On the way to the lighthouse, Mr Ramsay's daughter Cam begins 'to tell herself a story of adventure about escaping from a sinking ship'. She leaves it unfinished because the island for which they are bound does not offer rescue or the chance of survival. Neither does the one they have left behind. Cam gazes back at the settled reality of home and sees the abode of a living death: it looks, 'as if the people there had fallen asleep' or 'were free like smoke, were free to come and go like ghosts. They have no suffering there, she thought'. The voyage is undertaken 'in memory of dead people', the family members so casually eliminated earlier in the novel – Woolf spares only those seekers who set little store by life and prefer to scrutinize what lies beyond it. The painter Lily Briscoe, left behind on Skye, watches the boat vanish into the distance, 'swallowed up' by perspective until it becomes 'part of the nature of things', absorbed into a Lucretian flux. The end of the novel, commuting between two islands, balances two different kinds of annihilation. From the boat, those on forsaken Skye seem to be wandering in limbo. From the shore, those out to sea have been effaced by a vacancy that absorbs islands and blots out lighthouse beams.

A lighthouse on an island called Great Isabel watches over the harbour of an imaginary South American city in Joseph Conrad's novel *Nostromo*, published in 1904. The light in the tower, unbearably brilliant, is a deity ensconced in an expensive cathedral: 'the whole refracting apparatus, with its brass fittings and rings of prisms, glittered and sparkled like a dome-shaped shrine of diamonds, containing not a lamp, but some sacred flame'. Yet this sanctity has no power over the dark gulf it surveys, and it cannot console the sociable dandy Decoud, who suffers a moral and mental collapse when he has to hide out on Great Isabel for a few days to guard a hoard of silver. Deafened by silence, he drowns himself; the water is 'untroubled' when his body drops into it. Despite the divine beacon, Conrad's island is a place of execution. The all-seeing eye exposes Decoud's frailty, and within a few hours its scrutiny destroys him. *To the Lighthouse* disposes of this threat. At last, after so much talking and thinking, Woolf describes a physical motion that is heroic in its grand, perhaps suicidal, energy. As Mr Ramsay jumps ashore, his son James imagines him saying 'There is no God'. Although it is just a short step from the boat, he might be Nietzsche's Zarathustra leaping across a precipice and defying the abyss beneath. The mind completes its colonizing of open, empty space by ascertaining that there is no reason to be afraid; the journey ends in blank unconsciousness, not the revelation promised by Rachmaninov and Reger in their epilogues to Böcklin's painting.

To arrive at the island is to die, but it is also to disprove the existence of a retributive afterlife. We are at a literal dead end, debarred from proceeding further. As Lily Briscoe imagines the landing, she quotes another god dying on a cross and says out loud: 'It is finished'. She means that her painting of the scene is finished, as is the philosopher's exploratory venture into bleak, blank infinity. An island may, as Linnaeus suspected, be the first product of God's creation; an island is also where we discover the truth about a world that God long ago deserted.

<u>3.</u> NO MAN'S ISLANDS

In retrospect, the sense of alienation I felt in Tasmania was probably a gift to me. Because of their restrictions, islands stimulate curiosity and a fantastical wonder. Are there worlds elsewhere? And if so, how do those worlds complement or contradict each other?

The Greeks, who believed that all things must have a purpose, organized their scattered islands into something like a geometrical system. Delos, at the midpoint of the Cyclades, was given a divine provenance, placed under the protection of Zeus; this is where gods like Apollo or Artemis chose to be born. The outer islands were more secular, though they all had idols, temples, mythical genealogies. At the edge of the world, as reality wore thin and nature turned inhospitable, lay an imagined island populated by freaks and monsters, remnants of the chaos that preceded creation. This was Ultima Thule, identified at first with the British Isles, which – as classical geographers claimed – were situated inconveniently close to where the sea froze. During the Middle Ages, the location of the ultimate island was pushed further north or west: some maps placed it just off Scotland, others in Iceland or Greenland. On our spherical globe, space runs in a circle and therefore never runs out, but the Greek mind insisted on finitude, which obliged the world to finish at a specific point, marked by the full stop of a terminal island. In *The Odyssey*, the nymph Nausicaa says that in her sea-beaten home she and her people are 'the outposts of mankind', deprived of contact with other human beings. The cannibalistic Laestrygonians live on another frontier: their island lies in a region where day and night conjoin, perhaps close to the bronze door through which the sun makes its entries and exits.

The islands around the Greek mainland, fourteen hundred in all, became individually memorable when they were made into memorials. Naxos was where Ariadne pined after being abandoned by Theseus; it was on Lesbos that Sappho leapt from her cliff; and on Aulis, when the fleet was becalmed, Agamemnon sacrificed his daughter Iphigenia to the gods in return for a wind. Islands were apt settings for such calamities: geography imposed the inescapable unity of place that Aristotle saw as a formal requirement of tragedy. The victim was usually a woman, tethered to her island as if it were a determining fate. One man, Homer's Odysseus, was free to wander between the islands, spending time with Calypso or Circe or whoever the resident goddess happened to be, but always refusing to stay. In tragedy, an island is a situation from which there is no exit. Odysseus belongs to the different genre of romance, whose storytelling is digressive, elastic, potentially endless. The islands on which he pauses add to his dossier of experiences; he collects them, but is equally happy to let them go. He calls Ithaca the most western island, and associates it with the setting sun: it signifies rest, which is anathema to the mobile, deracinated hero. When he finally arrives home, he is brought to shore asleep, as if already enjoying a somnolent epilogue to life. Waking up, his first question to Athene is curious but revealing. After ten years at war and ten years on the journey back, he does not recognize his surroundings. He asks the goddess if this is one more improbable island, or could he be on the loamy mainland? She tells him he is in Ithaca, usually described by the poem as 'sea-girt'. His response is typically wily. He does not say that he is happy to be home; he simply tells her that he has heard of Ithaca, and is content to be adding another island to his list. In Phaeacia he introduces himself as a native of Ithaca, then immediately – muddling up geography, or perhaps being disingenuous – goes on to list the islands that lie east of his home: Dulichium, Same, Zacynthus. One of his eyes is always straying towards the horizon, on the lookout for further shores.

Odysseus is the first traveller in our literature. Every later wanderer cast up on an unknown island works through the itinerary of *The Odyssey*, but Homer tells the story in its archetypal form. The storms at sea that knock Odysseus off course are more than bad weather. He has offended the Olympian overseers of mankind, and they stir up tempests to wreck his ship. The vagaries of wind and water, directed by angry gods, throw him back onto the earth. But landfall usually means more suffering or a new danger. His first responsibility, as he dries himself and tests the ground beneath his feet, is to protect the fourth element, the spark of vitality within him. On the island of the nymph Nausicaa, almost dead from exhaustion, he creeps under a counterpane of fallen leaves to sleep. The poem compares him to a man in the wilds who protectively covers a burning log; he is, in Walter Shewring's translation, 'keeping alive the seed of fire'. That is his human duty, as a repository of the spark that Prometheus stole from the hearth of the gods and used to animate and enlighten the creatures he fashioned from the mud of the riverbed. The image is a reminder that a man on an island has to create civilization all over again. Later castaways all bother about making fire, and show every kind of ingenuity in their search for tinder or their use of burning-glasses. The Homeric image alludes to something more primal than keeping warm or being able to cook food: Odysseus kindles the spirit, ignites the inquisitive mind.

One of the first things he does on his islands is to climb to the highest point to make sure that he has the ocean all around him. This task too is obligatory for the literary castaways who follow him, but their aim is expedient: they want to find out if they can walk to safety. Odysseus is more disinterested. On the island of Aeaea he sends his companions off to do the humdrum work of reconnaissance, looking out for traces of human habitation. His reason for mounting the crag is not just to locate himself in the world; he has to discover which world he is located in.

Each new island has its Cyclops or Circe, a resident ogre or temptress who imposes rules that upset customary reality. In one place, men are killed and eaten like beasts; in the other, men are transformed into beasts, then kept as domestic pets. The bewildering succession of islands sabotages common standards, and suggests that humanity is simply the sum total of every possible kind of behaviour. Odysseus is the model of a classically versatile man who wants to savour every possible kind of life. On his travels, he becomes a dietary relativist. The Lotus Eaters, he discovers, subsist on fruit; Tiresias predicts he will visit a land whose people do not eat salted food. The experience of diversity is baffling, and the pace of his return to Ithaca slows down because he resists no detour, refuses no temptation. Warned to stop his ears against the deranging song of the Sirens, he finds a way of listening to them without risking self-destruction. The same skill at prevarication and compromise enables him to negotiate his way past the monsters Scylla and Charybdis, who menace him from opposite cliffs. He is subtle, shrewd, often dishonest; not single-mindedly heroic like the warrior Achilles, he remains open to contradiction.

Being a Greek, Odysseus wants to classify the novel phenomena he encounters, which means applying a binary logic to them. Is the Cyclops savage or tame, barbaric or hospitable? On Nausicaa's island, he acts as if both options might be simultaneously true: he emerges from his hiding place like a mountain lion defying its attackers, but uses a bough to cover his nakedness just in case he encounters civilized people. Meeting Nausicaa herself, he asks if she is heavenly or earthly. Every subsequent ardent man has repeated the question to ingratiate himself with a woman, but for Odysseus it is a genuine metaphysical query, not mere tactical flattery. Having identified two opposed categories, he avails himself of both. In the process he blurs or effaces his own identity, and escapes from the singleness that limits other men: he is not insular after all, because he can revise his own boundaries, assume new shapes, even – with the help of his protector Athene, who surrounds him with a mist – retreat into invisibility. Quizzed by the Cyclops, he nicknames himself Noman, Latinized as Nemo by some early translations. It is an apt alias, and he proves its truth by gripping the underbelly of a ram and merging with the beast to make his escape from the cave. He is indeed unlike other men, perhaps closer to the slippery mutability that gods enjoy.

In Cowper's translation, aesthetic synonyms for his guile abound. Circe recognizes him as 'Ulysses artifice-renown'd', and Alcinous worries that he might be a pretender,

> of whom no few
> Disseminated o'er its face the earth
> Sustains, adepts in fiction, and who frame
> Fables, where fables could be least surmised.

Islands are among the products of this gift for fabulation. They are facts moulded into fictions and strewn on the water like seeds. Artifice is necessary because myth is a story that can be told in opposite ways: the islands are alternately benign or treacherous, the journey of Odysseus is sometimes a quest and sometimes a wayward and irresponsible digression. Another symbol of this duality is Penelope's tapestry, woven by day and unwoven at night, perpetually renewed although no progress is ever made. In Cowper's translation the suitors watch her 'rav'ling the beauteous work'. They admire its 'subtlest woof': the web has texture, which means that it is made of entwined, over-lapping ingredients. In a pre-literary culture, *The Odyssey*, orally preserved and transmitted, is not yet a text, but this makes revision easier. There is no need for the labour of unravelling, since memory can omit or add whatever it pleases when the poem is next recited. In Homer's composition, islands perhaps serve as the warp, the stitch that, unlike the woof, goes backwards. They impede and decelerate the hero, and make it seem that he, like his wife with her tapestry, is going round in circles. Cowper's Ulysses refers to the traps Calypso and Circe set for him, yet insists that 'never could they warp my constant mind' – a tiny tribute to Penelope's artistry?

Both husband and wife are specialists in self-contradiction. They possess a rare and tricky talent, lost to human beings who make decisive choices and define themselves by anathematizing what they are not. Swift's hero in *Gulliver's Travels* is baffled, bemused and eventually deranged by the inconsistent realities he finds on the islands he visits: Lilliput with its midgets, Brobdingnag with its giants, the floating island with its population of air-headed philosophers. Gulliver's islands lie in the godforsaken region near Van Diemen's Land, and it's clear to him that God did not create any of them. But if there is no divinely upheld universal order to which he can appeal, his own human superiority is called into question. Odysseus, infinitely adaptable, suffers no such mental distress. The islands threaten his life, not his sense of who he is; he is no man in particular but potentially an Everyman. Gulliver confronts a more daunting existential quandary: estranged from his own species, is a man on an island a man at all? Robinson Crusoe saves himself from disorientation by constructing a little England. Odysseus, however, has no interest in putting down roots. The women who are the fixed points on his islands want to detain him because they have no share in his impatient imagi-nation, which is always advancing to the next stage. Although so much of *The Odyssey* is about sailing and the problems of navigation, the poem is able to

conceive of travelling without effort, using the mind to traverse space. Athene
tells Odysseus about the ships of the Phaeacians, which move as swiftly as
a bird in flight or a man thinking. Alcinous later explains the secret of that
speed: these vessels dispense with oars and steersmen and respond directly to
the promptings of intelligence, without involving the body's labour or relying
on wooden instruments. It is a wishful skill that many of us have inherited:
we can teleport ourselves to fantastical islands simply by mobilizing our
desire to be there.

Homer's islands encourage us to linger. The reader, beguiled by the book,
idles like Odysseus and his crew when the Lotus Eaters convert them to the
cult of satiety. But this dilatory tempo worried the neoclassical moralists
who took charge of the Greek legacy. In 1699 François Fénelon rebuked the
regressive stopovers made by Odysseus, and subsumed the poem's wayward
islands in a wider, more conscientiously organized community. In *Télémaque*,
Fénelon rewrote Homer's story as a critique of the spendthrift, luxuriant
Louis XIV, who shared the vices of Odysseus; his comments on the uses and
abuses of islands laid down rules of behaviour that were honoured throughout
the eighteenth century. In Rousseau's educational tract *Emile*, the young
hero is given *Robinson Crusoe* to read in adolescence, then *Télémaque* when
he becomes a man. No other books are necessary: between them they equip
Emile for existence. Defoe's novel, from this point of view, is about a child
constructing a private world. Fénelon deals with the more difficult adult
sequel to the games of the nursery, comparing different worlds and making
judgments about the ways of life they represent. Everything you need to know,
it seems, can be learned on an island.

Fénelon turned away from Odysseus to concentrate on his more upright
son, who retraces his father's route back from Troy. Telemachus is accompanied by his navigator Mentor, actually the goddess of wisdom, Minerva,

in disguise. This moral compass deplores the landfalls made by Odysseus in Sicily, Cyprus and Crete, which are the result of errant navigation or the caprice of winds; he steers Telemachus away from Cythera, where Venus plies him with perfumed liquors, and even builds a ship on which he can escape from the island of Calypso. When one of Calypso's jilted nymphs angrily burns the getaway boat, Mentor knocks Telemachus into the water and directs him to swim to safety. Allegorized by Fénelon, episodes in Homer become rehearsals for moral warfare. Mentor mobilizes Crete for combat, and the din of hammering and the seething of furnaces recalls 'that isle where Vulcan, animating the Cyclops, forges thunderbolts for the father of the gods'. Volcanic islands are not symptoms of a passionate upheaval below the surface, as they were for Byron; a volcano, in Fénelon's view, is nature's hard-working factory, cladding the earth in an armoured skin of lava as tough as iron, steel or brass. When Crete is first sighted, its mountains merge with the clouds and the waves in the kind of mirage that delighted voyagers in the South Seas. Is it an illusion, like the false, phantasmal Ithaca conjured up by Neptune to mislead Telemachus? Fénelon's description penetrates the poetic haze. Mount Ida separates itself from the murk and its summit comes into focus like the horns of an ancient, commanding stag, an image of crowned power and mental sovereignty. The coasts are banked like an encircling amphitheatre: nature instinctively imitates culture.

The island of Tyre is said to float on the waters without any firm foundation. But the islanders overcome this disadvantage by inventing navigation, which enables them to unite nations separated by the sea. Jupiter is partial to the Phoenicians, who have made the sea 'the bond of society'; Mentor tells a convocation of kings that mankind is a single family, and later calls the whole world a 'universal republic'. Republics are public spaces shared by all those who use them, so we must imagine the wastes of water – abridged by shipping, contracted by commerce – as a damper version of the Roman forum.

Fénelon's moral project would ideally extend to the abolition of islands: their local quirks interfere with the moral imperatives that make our planet a unitary place, a consistent and intelligible universe. Telemachus cites the existence of deserts as a reason for not making war, asking why men squabble over terrain, when so much of the earth remains vacant. (The argument could be applied to desert islands, sketch pads on which a group of men can design a society.) Diomedes begs the assembled Daunian chiefs to grant him a piece of land – cliffs or a stretch of sand would do, he says – so that he and his troops can construct a city, a melancholy replica of their lost home; they bestow on him the territory of Apri. This colonizing agenda was smuggled back into Homer's poem by Cowper, whose translation turned Ulysses into the kind of industrious settler of whom Fénelon approved. When he arrives in Calypso's domain, Cowper's Ulysses reflects that man 'might improve the peopled isle', whose 'unctuous glebe' could sustain vines and fruit trees. For Ulysses, even sailing is a surrogate form of agriculture, paradoxically attaching him to the earth rather than releasing him from its bonds. Cowper says that he 'plow'd again/ The spacious Deep', or 'thresh'd the brine': he is harvesting the water.

Later travellers, forgetting Mentor's strictures, followed in the tracks of Odysseus and repeated his mistakes. On his tour of the Hebrides in 1774, Samuel Johnson – who in principle shared Fénelon's view of islands, which he saw as places averse to cultivation and lacking social graces because they were miserably underpopulated – was relieved by some elegant hospitality he received on the island of Rasay. 'If I could have found an Ulysses,' he commented in his chronicle of the trip, 'I had fancied a Phaeacia.' He was joking about his credulity, and about his capacity for making the best of things: the house in which he was entertained hardly matched the bronze-walled palace of Alcinous, where the doors have silver lintels and handles of gold, with gardens in which figs, pomegranates and olives can be picked all year round.

Goethe, visiting Sicily in 1787, was more genuinely anxious to believe that he had wandered into the enchantments described by Homer. He thought that the public gardens of Palermo were surely 'the island of the blessed Phaeacians', and hurried off to buy a copy of *The Odyssey* so that he could check the resemblance; he sat in the gardens every day reading Homer and day-dreaming about Nausicaa – at least about her 'dramatic possibilities', since he planned a play about her infatuation with the enigmatic stranger who arrives in her land. Goethe fancied that he possessed a passing likeness to Odysseus. A wanderer far from home, he had an exotic allure for the locals, some of whom might consider him a demigod. Would he arouse desires like those that destroyed Nausicaa? Ordered to pay his respects to the despotic governor in Messina, he remembered the carnivorous hospitality of the Cyclops and secretly invoked his patron Odysseus, asking him to beseech the protection of Athene. The governor growled and glared, but made no attempt to eat Goethe. The tour had a scientific purpose: Goethe's aim was to investigate geological origins, which he studied by observing volcanoes, and to locate what he called the 'Ur-Pflänze', a primal organism from which all other plants may have germinated. His memories of Homer were equally archetypal, because they exposed the ancient grounding of his travels. He found, however, that mythic fancies were inconsistent with the sober discipline of botany: when he began to inspect the plants in Palermo – espaliered lemon trees, hedges of oleander, luscious red blossoms like carnations – he was instantly repatriated from 'the garden of Alcinous' to 'a garden of the natural world'. He lamented the dissecting obsession of 'we moderns', and pitied himself for being 'haunted and tempted by so many spirits'; at least those spirits were wisps of intellectual speculation, not the nymphs or carnal witches who distract Odysseus. Although Goethe worried about his errant theorizing, he persisted in his effort to connect poetry and science. One evening he admired an arc of cloud, gilded by the setting sun. His guide suggested that it extended from Sicily to Malta, and Goethe wondered if 'the mutual attraction between the two islands' might be made manifest atmospherically by that vaporous rainbow. The islands were bodies separated in space; the cloud revealed the yearning spiritual affinity between them.

In 1938 Nikos Kazantzakis published a poetic continuation of *The Odyssey* in which he dared to supersede Homer, to press beyond the borders of his world; the sequel establishes its bolder ambition by dismissing the Greek islands as unworthy destinations for a voyaging hero. While writing his epic, Kazantzakis made a trip to Japan, where the 940 islands in the Inland Sea reminded him of an 'all-blue Greece'. Asia occasionally confronted him with moral trials like those Odysseus undergoes. Venturing into a Singapore nightclub, he wondered if he should surrender to the Sirens who sang, danced and flirted there, while the bare islands around Hong Kong looked like sunning bodies after a swim, as if Calypso or Nausicaa had metamorphosed into clumps of curvaceous earth. Such temptations were easy to resist, because the journey convinced Kazantzakis that the travels of Homer's hero were as trivial and provincial as Leopold Bloom's wanderings through Dublin in Joyce's *Ulysses*. The Mediterranean, Kazantzakis declared in 1935, had dwindled to 'a local lake', as introverted as the Inland Sea; a new world had as its centre the Pacific Ocean, ringed by the antagonistic powers of China, Soviet Russia, the United States and Japan (which, despite its puny size, he called 'the fourth gorgon').

This expansion accounts for the itinerary of Odysseus in Kazantzakis's poem. Leaving Ithaca as Penelope sleeps, he churns all memories of the place in his head, then swallows and excretes those souvenirs. Later he dreams of a king who is enraged by the limitations of reality. 'My kingdom's but an island,' the madman exclaims as he runs round his circular domain, 'and the sea's its noose!' This is no precious stone set in a silver sea; water chokes the royal island, throttling it by denying access to a wider world. Odysseus is bound for the end of the earth – for the furthest point that the mind can reach. That ultimate goal may be the idea of God (an illusory goal, because the hero, no longer the plaything of Homer's gods, is for Kazantzakis their equal); or perhaps it is death, symbolized not by the black island that rears up before Dante's Ulysses but by the South Pole, the white, abstract hell which the modern Odysseus reaches as he expires. Such grandiose conceptual destinations need to be represented by continents, so Kazantzakis sends his hero down through Africa on a quest for the source of the Nile, then further south to Antarctica. Sailing on, Odysseus discounts the fictional, fantastic islands that might detain less determined seekers. An island of rosy coral with a cluster of palms beckons him; he does not pause. He briefly recalls the isles of the blessed with their warm breezes and grape harvests, but is content to be invigorated by the blizzards of the frozen continent, the unknowable region that lies outside our experience. He even sails past a snowy island whose inhabitants are ghosts. Death for him is not a place of rest, like the mausoleum in Böcklin's painting; it is another sequel, a further extension of his travelling. With his last breath he summons his shipmates to pick up speed, because 'Death's breeze blows in a fair wind!'

Kazantzakis had good reason for transferring the quest away from his homeland. In 1952 Jean Cocteau took a cruise around the Greek islands on a yacht named – in honour of the mythical poet he adopted as his self-image – *Orphée II*. To his dismay, he found the islands to be 'myth-scoured', crassly secularized by Catholic and Turkish invaders. He noted in his journal that 'the Greek islands are nothing but an idea one creates for oneself'. Their temples were derelict, because the gods had fled. There was no sign of them in the burnished summer sky, and the eroded terrain of the islands looked like a symptom of this spiritual depletion: the land resembled the worn hide of a donkey. Cocteau made an invidious comparison with Corsica, which at least was covered with 'green fur; it hasn't contracted alopecia'. The evidence

of geological catastrophe reminded him that the islands, as fall-out from
the earth's disastrous convulsions, had witnessed and perhaps enacted the
birth of Greek tragedy. After a recent eruption, the cone of the volcano on
Santorini still vomited sulphur and gypsum. That violence elated Cocteau:
'Here one suffers less from the anguish of being nothing'. Despite the desecra-
tion, there were still encounters with menacing Homeric ogres. Obstructive
officials searched luggage, presented forms that had to be filled in and charged
for permits. These modern versions of the Cyclops refused on principle to
accept the idealistic notion of a quest. The yacht's crew was harassed by questions about the reasons for the voyage; when they replied that their employer
simply wanted to visit the islands, the customs officers said, 'That is a mean-
ingless answer'.

The rich patrons who owned *Orphée II* pampered Cocteau and subsi-
dized his artistic projects, making him feel that he lived 'on a desert island
in the middle of our times'. Better to be Crusoe than Odysseus, especially
because the plight of the castaway – whose island now had sails, a motor and
an attentive crew of Fridays – had turned into an affluent privilege. He was
briefly heartened by a visit to Spetse, an aesthetic autocracy where 'ugliness
has never set foot'. The island was controlled by an entrepreneur who ensured
that visitors were wealthy and well-behaved; it housed an academy where, in
a revival of classical pedagogy, a hand-picked selection of Greek youths was
educated. 'Is it possible that such an island exists?' asked Cocteau. He fancied
that, when the vulgar democracy of France became intolerable, he might
'grow old here in one of these little white houses', safe from the visual irritation
of 'ridiculous shapes'. Then he found that ugliness had after all left its imprint
'in the form of a hotel – Istanbul-style'. He suffered a similar revulsion at
Knossos on Crete. 'Tonight,' he wrote in his journal, 'we shall escape – like
Theseus, like Ariadne, like Phaedra, like Daedalus and Icarus.' Freedom lay
away from islands, on the open, uncorrupted sea.

4 · A DESIGNED ISLAND

Travelling through Java in 1925, Aldous Huxley was entranced by what he called 'a process of cloud-making' that spun out across the tropical sky every morning. The air condensed into crags of vapour, which floated into the sky above the volcanoes. Then, as the result of some bubbling creative ferment, these fuzzy monoliths of humidity expelled new shapes from their summits – 'white islands' as Huxley called them – which drifted away across the hazy blue horizon.

Who would not enjoy daydreaming about a white island, a blank page not yet defaced by history? One such island has perennially enticed the imagination, although its proper home is not in the sky but beneath the sea. It is the Platonic island of Atlantis, described by a speaker in one of Plato's dialogues, and given the geometrical rigour that for him was the signature of a celestial intelligence. Critias tells Socrates that Atlantis was settled in concentric circles, with rectilinear canals that brought the sea inland. Huxley's islands of cloud never develop beyond provisional doodles, but Atlantis was a diagram, rectifying unruly nature. Critias says that an oblong plain surrounded the city at the centre of the island. But this planar surface did not satisfy the tidy-minded Atlantean kings, who corrected its defects by digging a trench around it to give it straight edges. Even the political system of the island deferred to numerical lore, which in Plato's view vouched for the orderly structure of the world. The regional kings, of whom there were ten, met at intervals in the temple of Poseidon; these assemblies took place every fifth and then every sixth year, to demonstrate respect for both odd and even numbers.

Fantastical islands where treasure is buried usually challenge us to locate them, but there is no chance of our ever finding Atlantis. Critias begins his exposition by saying that it capsized after an earthquake, leaving behind only the sludge that clogs the strait between the Pillars of Hercules and blocks entry to the ocean. The catastrophe is apparently the result of divine displeasure. The degenerate Atlanteans, corrupted by the precious metals they mine, are condemned by Zeus. In Plato's text, Zeus summons the other gods to hear him pronounce judgment, but then the narrative breaks off before the god starts speaking. Did Plato not write the rest because he refused to accept the verdict handed down from heaven? Or does the foundering of Atlantis reflect his personal disillusionment? The fate of the 'sacred island' may allude to his frustrated schemes to reform Sicily, where he was an unheeded adviser to the dissolute ruler Dionysius II. Yet even after it submerged, Atlantis could hardly be forgotten, if only because the measurements given by Critias made it less an island than a sixth continent, 'larger than Libya and Asia combined'. Readers of Homer shifted it back from the Atlantic and squeezed it into the Mediterranean, identifying some of the islands visited by Odysseus as relics of Atlantis. Archaeologists fancied that it might be Knossos, the citadel of Minoan Crete, ruined by an obscure disaster. Another explanation equated Atlantis and its hoard of minerals with the tin mines near Cádiz, close to the Pillars of Hercules, and interpreted the myth as a piece of shrewdly deceptive advertising. The Phoenicians, having taken control of the mineral trade, misled competitors by promoting the legend of a fabulously rich kingdom to the west; they then placed its wealth beyond the grasp of their rivals by sinking it beneath the waves. The enigmatic island, in this fable, took its treasure with it when it drowned.

The abstract images of perfection that Plato called Ideas hover above our gross material world, resisting realization. Atlantis, where gods and men consorted as equals, may have preserved its purity by dipping out of sight beneath the waterline. The Renaissance encouraged cerebral expeditions to salvage the philosophical island. In 1516 Thomas More designed his Utopia as a dredged-up Atlantis; its supposed discoverer is the explorer Raphael Hythloday, praised by More for the intrepid range of his travels, which far exceed those of Ulysses. Utopia is a realm to be governed, an arena for trying out radical laws about property and our shared obligations as members of a collective body. More's fable disparages Plato for having failed with Dionysius II, and he expects to be more successful in his own imaginary setting. Utopia is five hundred miles long, and tapers at both ends so that on a map, as Hythloday says, it resembles a new moon: it is a planet with room to grow as the mind progressively enlightens its shadowy side. In 1626 Francis Bacon imagined his own 'new Atlantis', an island called Bensalem. Utopia was an experimental commonwealth; Bensalem is more like an institute for scientific research. Its citizens are concerned with something profounder than social organization, and want to know why the world exists and how it functions. In an institution called Salomon's House they seek out 'the knowledge of Causes, and secret motions of things'. Plato's myth reproached the Greeks for having forgotten or betrayed their ideal origins: the island was the paradise they had lost. But Utopia and Bensalem are situated in the tantalizing future, not the irretrievable past. Rather than bemoaning our lapse, we can still aspire to live in this brainy Eden; the goal can be attained if we go on improving our intelligences. Insularity is a necessary scruple for both More and Bacon, because the place where the idea has its headquarters must be cordoned off from unrefined reality. Utopia has seceded from the mainland, thanks to the ditch-digging of its founder King Utopos. Bensalem maintains a strict moral quarantine: the wrecked sailors in Bacon's fable have to swear that they are law-abiding, and are sequestered by the authorities because some of them are ill. Isolation is a moral and spiritual privilege. The Bensalemites consider their island to be 'the virgin of the world', although that purity evinces 'the chaste minds of this people'.

Fictions like this anticipate Linnaeus's thesis that the world began on an island. Utopos churns up the earth and compels the sea to disgorge 'an isle that erst no island was', as if revising the topography of Genesis. Bacon's South Sea voyagers, adrift in 'the greatest wilderness of waters in the world', contrive their own variation on the biblical beginning. They pray, reminding God that he once 'discovered the face of the deep, and brought forth dry land'; next day, benefiting from an apparent miracle, they arrive at 'the port of a fair city'. But even when they land, they seem to be stranded between old and new worlds, unsure whether they have been claimed by death or lifted up into a better life. Flattering their hosts, they wonder if they have 'come into a land of angels'.

But are such islands the gifts of merciful heaven, as Bacon implies, or tributes to the human power of intellectual projection? A testimonial letter attached to Utopia answers the question by extravagantly commending More's 'notable, yea, almost divine wit'. Bacon's renovated Atlantis contains a College of the Six Days' Works where God's creative endeavours in the first week are elucidated by science, which defines the natural laws that even a deity must obey. Although Bensalem is devoted to 'enlarging the bounds of Human Empire', its imperial exploits focus on the accumulation of knowledge, not commercial gain. Ministers go abroad in secret to check on the learning of other nations and carry home whatever may be useful; these spies, called 'merchants of light', bring books back to Bensalem. Hythloday likewise bestows on the Utopians a more or less complete set of Greek and Latin classics and teaches them how to make paper and imprint letters, so they can graduate from scribbling on skins or on tree bark and produce extra copies of Plato and Aristotle. This emphasis on amassing a library strikes me as a little sad. The culture of these academic islands is not innate or native but has to be imported; I am reminded of the cardboard boxes of Victorian first editions – Ruskin, Meredith, Carlyle – which I found in a musty thrift shop in Hobart during my adolescence, all on sale for a few shillings. Who first brought them to Tasmania, and who else, after a few generations of handing down the inherited lumber, threw them away? Islands are self-enclosed, but can never be intellectually self-sufficient. Ideas need a larger space in which to circulate, and they flourish in a community that is quarrelsome because of its diversity.

Plutarch commented 'the only thing Plato ever left imperfect was the Atlantic isle': this was perhaps a mercy, because a perfect society will probably be a totalitarian one, run like a model prison. When More says that 'the whole island is as it were one family or household', for me it immediately turns into a dystopia from which I want to escape. After banishing private property, Utopia also does away with the right to privacy. The society lacks recesses of idleness or debauchery, because renegade Utopians are 'in the present sight and under the eyes of every man'. In Bensalem the same ocular regime is synonymous with science: Salomon's House is described as 'the very eye of this kingdom'. But the unblinking eye might just as well belong to a prison guard on St Helena or Alcatraz. As it happens, the perfecting of the idea is obstructed by the imperfect texts of More and Bacon. Hythloday can only bestow 'the most part of Plato's works' on the Utopians; the collection remains 'unperfect' because some volumes have been ripped to shreds by a pet monkey. New Atlantis concludes with a similar apology. Before the text runs out, it lists the achievements of Bensalemite science – which range from manufacturing rich compost to curing disease, from plastic surgery to the development of telepathic or tele-kinetic powers – but imparts no formulae that might be profitably put to use. A note by Bacon's secretary explains this evasion, which like Plato's retributive earthquakes and floods places the ideal beyond our reach: 'The rest was not perfected'.

Before this curtailment, Bacon sets a bold agenda for his techno-logical Atlantis. Nature here will be superseded by human invention. Plato's Atlanteans possess a metal called orichalc, almost as valuable as gold; it is a symbolic blessing that announces divine favour, and when the islanders start to be proud of their unearned wealth their downfall occurs. Bensalem needs no such benefactions. Its technicians boast of concocting artificial metals, which are used (though again no details are given) to prolong human life. Beyond this, Bacon's scientists transform reproduction into a matter of clini-cal engineering, and render the sloppy coition of bodies unnecessary. They generate plants 'without seeds', and hybridize animal species; 'by art' they produce fruit and flowers that are 'greater much than their nature'. To us, all this suggests the genetic modification of foodstuffs or the production of synthetic substances like plastic. Bacon had no such misgivings. The scientific innovations he lists allude to the grand competitive project of the Renaissance: the attempt to demonstrate that man can literally recreate the world. Plato's Atlanteans were of divine stock, though intermarriage with mortals adulter-ated this bloodline. The Bensalemites, however, are God's rivals – creators, not abject and submissive creatures.

On Prospero's island in *The Tempest*, magic speeds up the inductive trial and error of Bacon's laboratories. Nature succumbs to art when Prospero picks up his wand and gives orders to the elements. But rather than waiting for a judgment from above like that pronounced by Plato's Zeus, or deciding not to complete the story like Bacon, Shakespeare's magus renounces sorcery, asks forgiveness for appropriating powers that are more than human, and quits his disenchanted domain. His charms, as he says when he gives them up, resemble clouds – white bubbles of thought like those Huxley saw in Java, conjured up by white magic. The ideal island preserves its secrets by retreating towards the horizon or dissolving into air, thin air.

According to the Greek historian Diodorus Siculus, Atlantis preserved the earliest records of the world's creation; in the absence of reliable history, myth takes over to reconnect us with the source. Late in the seventeenth century, a physician called Olaus Rudbeck claimed that the mythical kingdom was Sweden, the uncredited progenitor of European civilization. William Blake liked to imagine the ocean solidifying in 'Atlantean hills' to unify the sundered family of man, scattered between Europe and America. D. H. Lawrence entertained similar dreams of a paradisial time when the oceans were plains on which 'the soft, dark-eyed people of that world could walk round the globe'. The theosophist Madame Blavatsky believed that the temples and libraries of Atlantis were the repository of arcane wisdom, and even today the therapist Elisis Livingstone – who ministers to the credulous at her Shambhala Retreat in Glastonbury, in the south of England – reminisces about 'our Atlantean past', when we apparently had twelve strands of DNA not two. A druidic website continues to mourn the lost kingdom and its precocious technology. The Atlanteans, it insists, were like amphibious Martians – extraterrestrials equipped with supercomputers on which they plotted planetary movements. Mystics like to see the Hebridean island of Iona as an outcrop of Atlantis that still crests the waves, while another legend disseminated on the internet outlines an even more extended divine pedigree, claiming that Atlantis was colonized by the polar Hyperboreans, a race that descended to earth from the Sirian galaxy.

Rather than being lost in the past, Atlantis offers a visionary glimpse of the future, when men, by the exercise of intellect, may perhaps re-establish their kinship with the gods. In 1874 the myth made one of its intermittent returns to the surface in Jules Verne's scientific romance *The Mysterious Island*. During the American civil war, a hurricane buffets five men and a dog in a hot-air balloon across the Pacific; they crash-land on a volcanic island, where – led by the engineer Cyrus Harding – they construct a civilization more technically advanced than the one they have left behind. Atlantis is their model. Harding surmises that islands like theirs are the peaks of a sunken continent that once formed a sixth of the known world; the Pacific is more likely to have swallowed such a landmass than the narrower Atlantic. As if copying the man-made topography of Plato's Atlantis, Harding foresees a system of industrial canals that will transport the metals he and his companions mine. In time he hopes that these sluggish channels will be augmented by railways – 'yes, railways! Of which a network would certainly one day cover Lincoln Island'.

In *Robinson Crusoe* the wrecked ship provides the castaway with the implements and supplies he needs for building and stocking a house, as well as the weapons to defend it. Verne's characters, on the other hand, smuggle in no such advantages; they lack the tools necessary for making tools, and cannot boast so much as a knife. When they turn out their pockets they discover a notepad and a single match, with which they re-enact the kindling of fire by Prometheus – the first mental transgression, the act that allowed men to form a society and develop a culture. Otherwise the only equipment they possess is Harding's ingenious brain, which in its reticulated compartments contains the sum of all human knowledge. Crusoe has his Bible, to be consulted in emergencies; Verne's men possess instead the indexed, orderly mind of their leader, who like an infallible book answers all their questions. Under his guidance, they go back to the beginning of human culture, then during their fifteen years on the island advance at speed through its ensuing stages. They dig up clay and fire earth in a kiln to make pottery. They gouge quarries, extract metals and, after hunting seals and using their skins as bellows, manufacture hot lumps of iron ore that they hammer into spades and axes. They shear the indigenous animals they trap, wash the greasy wool in baths of soda, then press and weave cloth. Harding assembles the ingredients for making a battery, and prepares to generate electricity. Since the members of Verne's team are all male, they cannot increase and multiply in the biblically ordained manner. Undiscouraged, they rely on their owns means of mechanical reproduction: they happen upon a photographic apparatus, complete with chemicals – a violation of the rule that deprives them of external technical help – and take portraits of each another. 'It multiplies us,' one of them remarks about the camera.

Bacon's Bensalemites defer to 'the great Atlantis (that you call America)'. Verne's colonists, transferring Atlantis to another ocean, vow to make 'a little America of this island!' They name it after the current President, which is their way of wishfully annexing it to the United States. Although they hope to provide the republic with a stepping-stone for its conquistadorial advance across the Pacific, a volcanic eruption upsets their plans; they return home and re-establish their industrial Atlantis on dry land in a vacant corner of Iowa. The island, meanwhile, has disintegrated after a volcanic eruption, like Krakatoa in 1883. No angry god need be blamed for the calamity. Harding's science, commandeering the elements and violently interfering with the dull stability of nature, employs destruction as a creative technique. He topples a granite cliff with a home-made brew of sulphuric acid and nitroglycerine. One of his subordinates asks if he intends to blow up the island. He could do so if he wished, and when he fires the volatile chemical 'the island appeared to tremble to its very foundations', with stones hurled around as if the restive crater were already having its tantrum. The final cataclysm might be another of Harding's pyrotechnical stunts.

Verne's Atlantis is not punished from on high, like Plato's island; its fate is determined by the unbridled energy of the mind, whose quest for first

causes and for the secrets of cosmic structure is bound to end in an attack
on the opaque, obstructive material world. During the twentieth century,
the American psychic Edgar Cayce argued that Atlantis had tumbled into
the Caribbean, with the Bimini Islands as the tips of its sunken mountains.
Events on Atlantis, chronicled by Cayce during mystical trances, followed a
plot seemingly borrowed from science fiction, with the diabolical progeny of
Belial fighting the Sons of the Law of One for control of subhuman toilers
called Things. Their war was about energy, stored in a crystalline stone as
occult as Plato's orichalc. Like an overheated battery, the crystal set off the
explosion that caused Atlantis to capsize.

    In 1908 Anatole France's satire *Penguin Island* anticipated this warning
about redesigning the geography of Genesis or defying the edict of Plato's
Zeus. A myopic Breton monk drifts out into the Atlantic on a block of stone
that has come loose from the continent, and when he comes to an archipelago
of ice he whimsically baptizes a colony of penguins. God, seeking to rationalize this improper use of the sacraments, converts the birds into humans; the
monk tows their island back to the Breton peninsula with a fine cord of flax.
But the change of species is bad for the temper of the peaceable, pottering
birds, which begin to squabble with each other. The end comes with a terrorist
bombing: divine rage is replaced by the ideological insanity of the human race.
A character called Professor Obnubile quits the doomed island and crosses
to America, 'the new Atlantis', where he expects the future to be on view.
He was probably disappointed: soon after migrating to New York in 1939,
W. H. Auden wrote a poem called 'Atlantis', which warns that you can only sail
there in the Ship of Fools and will never arrive. Why not stay safely, miserably
at home and 'peep at Atlantis/ In a poetic vision'? Now that we know what lies
beyond every horizon, it is hard to believe that an undiscovered paradise might
materialize in the haze. America no longer qualifies as our ideal Atlantis, and
Verne's febrile factories are not proof of human perfectibility. The Atlantean

dream has been left to psychotic magnates like Lex Luthor, who in Bryan Singer's film *Superman Returns* detonates bombs in the middle of the Atlantic and piles up the debris in basalt columns that will support a new metropolis. Lois Lane asks if he is building an island. 'No,' he huffily replies, 'a continent' – a substitute for fallen America, which will be scuttled by his explosions. Zeus should rebuke such hubris; instead Superman whirls down to confound Luthor, and the artificial island sinks again into a dyspeptic ocean.

5. GOD'S OUTPOSTS

Islands lie at the edges of a world we think we know, and the gaps between them make that perimeter porous: can they mount a defence against the bogeys, demons or rival deities assembled beyond the border? Bacon's travellers are relieved to discover that Bensalem has been converted to Christianity, although they wonder how a place so far 'from the land where our Saviour walked' came to be redeemed. Truth, they are told, arrived in about AD 50, announced by a pillar of light topped with a glowing cross. This luminous column broke apart and dispersed into a starry galaxy; below on the water floated an ark – 'not wet at all… though it swam' – containing a Bible and a testimonial personally written by St Bartholomew. A messenger conveniently calls the governor of Bensalem away before he can be questioned on the gospel's bewildering arrival. But the sailors are eager to believe him, because there is now no need to confront the infidel.

On its advance through the Roman Empire, Christianity used overland routes rather than taking to the oceans like Bacon's ark. But when the imperial territory reached its ragged terminus in the Hebrides, the evangelists ran into an older faith that used the islands as its redoubts. There were druidic altars on

Iona; in the sixth century St Columba established a monastery there to train missionaries for the work of conversion. Holy Isle, off the Scottish coast near Arran, was the preserve of a Celtic water sprite; St Molaise, whose hermitage was a cave near a healing well, drove out his infidel predecessor and established the island's reputation for washing away bodily distempers and curing the soul's malaise. After a visit from the heathen Vikings and centuries of occupation by unspiritual sheep farmers, Holy Isle was sanctified all over again in the 1990s, when it became the home of a Buddhistic community dedicated to global peace and ecological harmony. The freehold changed hands after a convergence of dreams. Practising yoga during an American retreat, Lama Yeshe had a vision of an island that might function as a meditative retreat; the Catholic wife of the previous owner was ordered to sell it to him by the Virgin Mary, who visited her during the night to advise about the disposal of her estate. In 1877 the Stevenson family of engineers had built a lighthouse on Holy Isle: with its paraffin lamp, this was the emblem of another faith – or of no faith in anything but the omniscience of the scientific mind. Now a square tower with an electric flare radiates what Lama Yeshe calls Inner Light. The cottages once occupied by lighthouse keepers serve as monastic cells, where members of the community immure themselves for periods lasting from three months to three years.

St Aidan, travelling from Iona, founded a monastery on Lindisfarne, linked to the Northumbrian coast by a narrow causeway. High tide washes over this land bridge but leaves the island above water: the monks took this to be God's guarantee that the faithful would survive the apocalypse. As on Holy Isle, the Christian sanctuary suffered an assault from the Vikings; Henry VIII dissolved the Benedictine monastery, but a Presbyterian church was built in the nineteenth century, and Catholicism later re-established a foothold. Havens are still available on Lindisfarne for those who wish to calm and chasten their minds, but the modern world has caught up. The car park is usually choked, and minibuses ferry visitors from one sacred site to the next. Because the island is so cramped, it has had to universalize itself: the Lindisfarne Community is a network of home-based churches scattered across the United States, New Zealand and South Korea. Some of its members honour the island's memory by living as solitaries, 'seeking God "in the way of the desert"'. Others are exponents of what they call 'secular monasticism', which reinterprets the rules of denial and reclusion by allowing marriage and engagement with the world of work. The Abbess electronically ministers to her flock from the community's mother-house in upstate New York; she is a former dental therapist, who declares that she 'loves feminist theology, swimming and her two little non-human companions, Candy and Spartacus' – poodles as it happens, not elves or imps. The Abbot, her husband, plays a custom-made Celtic drum and an acoustic guitar, and – rebelling against the tyranny of trousers – likes to wear a kilt. Rather than living in poverty and preaching as he wanders the land, he is a tenured philosopher at a local university.

Alcuin, an adviser to Charlemagne, rallied the Lindisfarne monks to defend 'the camp of God' against the Viking raiders at the end of the eighth century. But Walter Scott saw the Orkney and Shetland Islands as disparate fragments of Scandinavia, where people who were proud of their Viking stock secretly revered the warfaring spirits of the Nordic sagas. In Scott's novel *The Pirate*, a cape on Zetland, destined in time to become 'a lonely mountain islet', is described as 'the terminating extremity' of the mainland. The phrase has its own fraught extremism: this terminus – the vanishing point of speculation like 'the Thule of the ancients' – is where God ought to be positioned. But Scott finds only emptiness, ruled by the unhallowed turbulence of the elements. On these 'wild islands', atavistic urges soothed by Christianity can still be gratified. The residents of Zetland in *The Pirate* worship elemental force, which prompts them to wreck passing ships and bludgeon the survivors. When Samuel Johnson toured the wind-battered western islands of Scotland, he scoffed at the absence of trees, which to him signified the impossibility of agriculture and of cultivated manners. Scott's characters disagree: they despise trees, and mock the improvers who want to plant them. A windbreak would muffle the storms that are the invigorating tantrums of their savage gods. A Norn poetically whips up a gale, and the heroine Minna, who calls herself 'a daughter of the old dames of Norway', is a warrior-maiden like Wagner's Brünnhilde. Avid for battle, unafraid of blood, Minna is infatuated by a pirate because he reminds her of the rapacious Vikings.

After a shipwreck, a survivor is seen clinging to a plank that whirls in the frothing water and then grounds itself on a 'small projecting spot of stones, sand, and gravel'. The man who grips the fragment of wood is already an islander, adrift alone on an unstable, unfounded scrap of ballast; Zetland too, whose inhabitants are more likely to attack him than to offer help, is an extension of that small tempest-tossed platform. The presence of those Celtic hermits or the beatifically serene Buddhists who are their descendants cannot pacify a region where the eroding earth is at the mercy of what Scott calls 'the hideous combustion of the elements' – agitated air and frenetic water, so crazed that they seem to have caught fire. Virginia Woolf's philosopher sets foot on an island to prove the non-existence of God. Scott's islands have resident gods, but they are the wrong ones.

The mind is best purged in a desert, like the arid waste between the Nile and the Red Sea to which St Anthony retired in the third and fourth centuries. As Christianity moved progressively northwest, it left such blistering vacancies behind; for Aidan and Molaise, a deserted island came to serve the same meditative purpose. In an age that has abandoned belief, islands still test our psychological fortitude. The modern equivalent of a spiritual trial is internal and invisible, but it can be made real if it happens on an actual island and is documented on film.

In 1949 Roberto Rossellini filmed *Stromboli* on a meagre island off the north coast of Sicily with an active volcano at its peak. He subtitled the film *Terra di Dio*, which is perhaps too easily allegorical: can the biblical creator be held responsible for this gaunt, smouldering place? When the volcano erupts, the islanders evacuate and sleep out at sea in their boats; a priest leads a service of thanksgiving as the congregation bobs on the water, but they should be propitiating Vulcan not the Christian God. The deity domiciled on Stromboli is given to fulminating, and seems to enjoy looking down on a massacre: after the fishermen trap their seasonal catch of tuna in an orgy of squirting blood and flailing foam, they doff their caps to chant grateful praises to Jesus and Mary. Ingrid Bergman plays a Lithuanian refugee, rescued from a displaced persons' camp by an Italian soldier who takes her home to Stromboli. She loathes the island, even though it mirrors her own insulated nature: Rossellini described the film as an attack on the aggressive self-will fostered by the war, which left survivors locked in grasping solitude like famished animals. She leaves her husband and walks off to sail back to the mainland; but to get to the port she has to trudge round the cone of the volcano. The hot rocks torment her feet, and fiery gusts of wind batter her. She has a glimpse of the molten core, like a foresight of perdition. Unable to advance, she spends the night on the crater; next morning, suddenly repentant, she cries out to merciful God and begs for strength to resume the life allotted to her. Mercy, however, is meant to drop from heaven like gentle rain, not in a blitz of scorching boulders, and it is hard to believe that Bergman can make peace with Stromboli's clannish society and narrow-minded religion. Despite the gratuitous blessing at the end of the film, Rossellini seems to have equated God with the harsh truth of photographic documentation. He said that he directed the camera to 'haunt and pursue' his characters, who cannot 'escape the unblinking eye of the lens'. Bergman is pinioned on the island like the hooked and netted fish, and her panic lays bare the distemper of the modern self.

At least there is a restive deity inside that burning mountain. A decade later in *L'Avventura*, Michelangelo Antonioni chose Lisca Bianca, an island in the same Aeolian group off Sicily, as an emblem of God's demise – or of his petrification into a stony totem, as indifferent as the statues on Easter Island. Lisca Bianca is hardly an island, more a spar poking out of the sea. It was once a volcano, but its fires, unlike those of Stromboli, have long been extinct: this inactivity is Antonioni's warning that there will be no adventure in his film, no climactic and cathartic eruption like the one that sears Bergman. On a yacht cruising through the archipelago, a fatuous socialite complains that the islands depress her, because they look bereft and abandoned. Having nothing better to do, her friends land on Lisca Bianca, as if their presence might cheer up this morose, sterile mound. On a ramble through the landscape of angular stones and dwarfish shrubs, a young woman belonging to the party unaccountably disappears. Her father rules out suicide, because – as he self-deceivingly notes – she had a copy of the Bible in her luggage. She is never found, and the searchers soon forget who they are looking for. This isle of the dead has expunged a woman who was no more than a weightless pleasure-seeker, even lighter than the air into which she vanishes. Another passenger on the yacht, reluctantly diving with scuba gear, refuses to believe that man originally lived in the sea. But *L'Avventura* confirms this theory of our origins: islands break up the liquid continuum of things, and are bound, like the woman who apparently dissolves rather than drowning, to be reabsorbed into the water.

The search is a series of short stories that soon reach dead ends. The island is not deserted after all: they find a hut (custom-built by Antonioni's crew), with an old man living in it. He claims to be a shepherd, even though his sheep are nowhere to be seen. A member of the party clambers out of a cleft in the rock holding half of an ancient urn, and reports that a Roman city is buried beneath the piles of boulders. A woman pleads to be given the vase, to use as a planter for her geraniums. One of the men handles it appraisingly, then accidentally lets it drop. It breaks into shards on the stone; he shrugs and they wander away. The Aeolian group takes its name from an allusion to *The Odyssey*, and Stromboli has been often been identified as the lair of the wind-god Aeolus. But in 1961 Antonioni dismissed such legendary prototypes as cumbersome 'baggage': better to travel light like his rootless, ephemeral heroine. He went on to complain that our myths – the stories we tell to exemplify moral force and investigate ultimate meanings – are still 'those that prevailed at the time of Homer'. This heritage falls away when he strips Lisca Bianca of its numinous aura. What happens there is absurd without being mysterious; the missing woman cannot levitate like a saint, so she simply evaporates.

Left undefended, God's offshore bastions are liable to be taken over by other spirits. These may be demons, at large because no Christian exorcist has expelled them, or perhaps they are only the private terrors that assail a man who chooses to live in solitude. During the 1960s Ingmar Bergman discovered Fårö in the Baltic, which became his reclusive bolt-hole. It offered him uterine security: he likened it to a womb, and from within this enclosure he could ponder bleak infinity – a sea crusted with ice, a glaring sky – and survey a world into which he had not yet been born. What if he stamped to and fro on the rocky beach, ranting to display his theatrical temperament? 'A gull, at most, would take off.' Castaways are usually dismayed by nature's unheeding response to their outcries; Bergman found this neutrality soothing. Out in the water, ancient gods kept watch with blind eyes. Stone slabs had been positioned there by the earliest residents, and the steles looked to Bergman like 'idols raising their heavy foreheads against the waves and the darkening horizon'. The foreheads were heavy, too dense to be capable of thought or feeling. The upright tablets testified to a human presence that acknowledged its own intrusive irrelevance.

Bergman chanced upon Fårö in 1959 while location-scouting for *Through a Glass Darkly*, which he at first wanted to make in the Orkneys. The film begins idyllically enough, as four happy laughing people wade out of the water, climb onto a jetty, and resume their separate lives on the island. They are exemplifying the theory that offends the diver in *L'Avventura*: we originate in the sea, in the ocean of collective unconsciousness, and when we reach dry land we attain the insulated state which we think of as individuality. The family in *Through a Glass Darkly* shares a summer home, but – as the schizophrenic heroine remarks – they occupy separate, incommunicable cubicles inside it. Karin herself, during her visionary fits, breaks out of this false shelter and escapes from the bordered, limited identity that vouches for sanity. She feels able to walk through walls, peeling back wallpaper like foliage. Wracked by anxiety, she takes refuge in a gutted ship, a Russian salmon-cutter that rusts on the shore. She curls up foetally in its half-submerged bowels, like Bergman in his womb: birth is a shipwreck, as J. M. Barrie said, and she regrets that she was ever marooned inside the self. She finally announces that she cannot go on commuting between two worlds; she agrees to be airlifted to a hospital on the mainland, though she refuses psychiatric treatment. To live on an island – as her husband, brother and father continue to do – is to be confined to your own head, like a monk in his study or a prisoner in his cell. Karin cannot accept this incarceration. Or is she not strong enough to tolerate a lifetime of her own company?

Hour of the Wolf, released in 1968, returns to the subject of insular insanity, alluding – as the initial case-history explains – to the mental disintegration of a painter living on 'the Frisian island of Baltrum'. The German island is a decoy, since the story refers once more to Bergman's voluntary isolation on Fårö, where he lived with the fanged tormentors that ran riot in the stories he filmed. Johan and Alma, played by Max von Sydow and Liv Ullmann, are seen arriving by boat with their possessions: art supplies, easels, frames and a potted plant. Importing the ideas of culture and cultivation, they intend to rationalize wildness as Prospero does with his wand and Crusoe with his gun, axe and Bible. But a native population of guerillas resists the aesthetic colonists. Johan calls these unseen imps cannibals, as if they were the kin of Shakespeare's Caliban; during one of his hallucinations, they metamorphose into birds that rip his flesh with their beaks. Rather than subduing the guerrillas, he is lured into complicity with them. A gloating demon presents Johan with a gun, with which he threatens the faithful Alma. It would be useless against the malevolent spectres that taunt him: you can only shoot spirits with a camera. Alma tracks the deranged Johan into the forest, where, like Anna in *L'Avventura*, he simply disappears. Telling her story to an unseen film-maker, she asks how it was that she too, during this last inconclusive journey, could see the goblins. But she is not addressing an analyst or therapist; the person behind the camera is a ghost inside a machine. Film is another kind of sorcery, not a means of elucidation.

Like Johan, Bergman went to ground on Fårö. The local people, when questioned by tourists, protectively insisted that they had never heard of him. He employed imaginary monsters as guards, and in front of his house displayed a notice warning 'Killer Dog – Keep Out'. (Needless to say, his actual dog was a harmless pet.) He even provided his attendant demons with a playpen by converting an old barn into a private cinema, a blacked-out sanctum where they could frolic during the hours of daylight: the cave of St Molaise had been electrified.

The spiritual life requires sacrifices, which have value in proportion to the pain they cause us. Stromboli offers a harsh and humbling moral education; Lisca Bianca exposes the desolate truth of our inhospitable world; Fårö leaves the artist alone with his menagerie of devils. But do islands need to be places of penance? In our secularized world, holy days have turned into holidays;

although islands remain favoured destinations, we travel there in quest of sun not enlightenment, and we rely on the sea rather than Molaise's sacred wells to cleanse and refresh us. Yet the most approachable and urbanized islands can still be invested with the glow of rapture that once radiated from Iona or Lindisfarne. In 1936 a new railway line from London to Portsmouth made possible quick connections to the ferry that crossed five miles of water to the Isle of Wight. A documentary film called *The Way to the Sea* commemorated the achievement, with a terse, jaunty score by Benjamin Britten and a reflective commentary by Auden.

A few years later the poet disparaged those who believed they could book passage to Atlantis on an ocean liner. His narration for the film is more indulgent. The trippers are latter-day pilgrims, and on their way to the baptismal sea they speed past the emblems of a new religion in which electricity is the demiurge – factories like white cathedrals, pylons with coils and wires that have 'power to create'. Having reached the coast, they are still not satisfied; now, in a subconscious choral chant, they announce: 'We seek an island'. Auden quickly categorizes them as they troop up the ferry's gangplank. Some are lonely, while others, trapped in tedious marriages, want to be alone; the two conditions are very different. They all hope to find a cure for what ails them on 'the pleasant island', but they are more like a queue of Freudian patients than the questers who sought absolution on Iona or Holy Isle. They are going, after all, to the last place in Britain to succumb to Christianity: this recidivist island, so close to the south coast, held out until the end of the seventh century. Most of Auden's travellers are on the lookout for some sort of erotic fillip. Although the Isle of Wight is not Cythera, its specialized array of pocket-sized landscapes – cliffs and golf courses, royal parks and snuggled villages – can cater to what his prose poem calls 'all the varieties of pleasure, permission and condolence'. Narcissists undress and parade their bodies, while the sedentary and the shelved vegetate in deck chairs. Children romp, enjoying 'the happiness of the immediate present'. Auden sends them all on their way with an ecumenical blessing that takes its cue from the benign subtitle of a Shakespearian comedy: 'Do what you will. … Be a sport or an angel. … Accept your freedom'.

With its whale skeletons, dinosaur bones and legendary pirates, the Isle of Wight still gallantly strives to keep up with the expectations of its visitors. It began fictionalizing itself in the 1840s when an entrepreneur opened an amusement park at Blackgang Chine: here you can now reel from a tropical jungle to a cowboy town in the American West, from a smugglers' cave to Sleeping Beauty's castle. Though Auden promised that the island would not disappoint those who have faith in its charms, his tender assurance has been sabotaged by a sly, agnostic irony that articulates the mood of our own times. Postcards now cheerfully advertise the Isle of Wight's famous frauds: Needles you can't thread because they are stumps of chalky rock, Cowes that can't be milked because cattle have been replaced by yachts, a town called Ryde where you have to walk or drive. Miracles should not be expected, here or on any other island. Our cult of leisure is like the religions it has supplanted: the bliss it purveys depends on our capacity for self-deception.

6. THE ART OF ISLAND-MAKING

By the early seventeenth century, islands were like coinage – the small change of continental exploration, easily amassed and idly spent. Shakespeare's Cleopatra remembers that Antony let realms and islands spill from his pockets like plate, by which she means pieces of silver. In fact Rome had little interest in collecting islands, because its empire marched overland rather than across the seas; Cleopatra's admiring, elegiac remark refers instead to the profiteering voyages of the Renaissance. In Shakespeare's early comedy *The Two Gentlemen of Verona*, Proteus is frustrated because his father keeps him idle at home, not allowing him to go to university or enlist as a soldier. A third career is likewise blocked: he cannot rove on the seas and 'discover islands far away', which is in itself enough to make a man a hero. To discover islands was a legitimate goal, because there were still islands aplenty waiting to be discovered.

The most ambitious explorers had continents in view; stray islands merely cropped up along the way, incidental and expendable. Columbus, imagining that he was bound for India, instead happened upon his own new Atlantis in the west; in the process he stumbled across the prolific Bahamas, all seven hundred of them. Later, ships blown off course by bad weather on their way to the English colony in Virginia found a haven in what we call Bermuda, a singular name that stretches across more than a hundred islands. Sir Martin Frobisher set out to find a northwest passage to the rich East, but had to content himself with the glacial slab of Baffin Island. Because islands were prizes, rival claimants squabbled about prior rights. Throughout the seventeenth century, Dutch and British sailors quarrelled over who first set foot on the Falkland Islands. In a time when geography was still provisional, wishful thinking occasionally got in the way of observation. California was initially mistaken for an island, and was believed to be a legendary celestial paradise ruled by Queen Califa. Hence its name, which comes from *The Exploits of Esplandian*, one of the chivalric romances that are blamed for addling the wits of Don Quixote; Esplandian's California is an island 'very close to the Earthly Paradise', where, since a mundane heaven is expected to be affluent, the only metal is gold. The Spanish expeditions that charted its lower end in the 1530s and 1540s established that Baja California was a peninsula. The explorers might have made the same deduction if they had ventured further north and mapped the edges of the peninsula that now has San Francisco at its tip. California is a state with the mentality of an island, as disjunct as Manhattan from the flat-minded American heartland; the San Andreas fault is a reminder of the secessionist itch that runs through all continents.

These acts of exploration were a quest for the unknown, the imaginary. Hence the mercenary dream of El Dorado, or the rumours about a land ruled by Amazonian female warriors. Cartographers, who established definitive borders and pinned wayward islands down in space, sometimes disparaged these fancies. Spain colonized the Canary Islands in the early fifteenth century; they retained the fantastical name given to them by the Romans, who were convinced that the islands were overrun by feral dogs or 'canes'.

The annotations to an atlas drawn in Mallorca in 1375 dismissed the legend identifying the Canaries with the Fortunate Isles, where Pliny the Elder claimed that 'the gifts of the earth can be harvested without sowing'. Nor were the Canaries, the atlas added, the place to which the soul is repatriated after death – though retirees who still settle there to enjoy paradise before death might disagree. Unabashed, the myth migrated into fiction: the second edition of *Utopia* contained a letter to More from Guillaume Budé assuring the author that his non-place or good place was 'one of the Fortunate Isles, perhaps very close to the Elysian Fields'. Donne transferred both the actual and mythical islands to a carnal map when he described a woman's lips as fortunate isles, 'Not faynte Canaries, but Ambrosiall'. No man is allowed to be an island, but for Donne a woman's body contained insular recesses that invited occupation. Other voyagers reported that the fancy had migrated west, to find a home among the many new worlds for which maps were hastily making room. In 1610 the *True Declaration of the State of the Colonie in Virginia* called the Bermudas 'those infortunate (yet fortunate) Ilands' – unpropitious because rocky, and because they were allegedly populated by devils; fortuitously friendly because a storm-battered fleet had found shelter there.

Classical prototypes were stretched to fit these supernumerary islands. Luís de Camões, describing Vasco da Gama's journey around the Cape of Good Hope in his epic poem *The Lusíads*, took the Cape Verde islands to be the blissful garden of the Hesperides, tended by nymphs at the western limit of the world. When the Romans co-opted the fable of Atlantis, they told stories about two phantasmal islands jointly called Antilia, beatific resorts with a mild, smiling climate, where the cultivation of the ground required no labour. After the Moors conquered the Iberian peninsula in the eighth century, the Portuguese looked to Antilia as a mythical refuge for imperilled Christianity. They called it the Island of the Seven Cities, ruled by bishops who had escaped from the infidel. Myth is about variability and adaptation, so mythmakers enjoy fabricating synonyms: the seven cities accordingly were called Aira, Anhuib, Ansalli, Ansesseli, Ansodi, Ansolli and (in an odd disruption of the alliterative riff) Con. After so much mental effort, it was a shame to waste the idea. Therefore, when Columbus discovered the West Indies, the archipelago dispersed across the Caribbean Sea was called the Antilles.

Explorers probed a border between daydreaming fancy and hardheaded acquisition; fabulation extended into an inventory of wealth that was literally fabulous, able to perform miracles. *The Lusiads* is an inventory of imperial spoils, with every island visited by Vasco da Gama making its own suppliant donation to the wealth of Portugal. Japan offers silver, Borneo camphor. Timor supplies sandalwood, the Maldives coconuts. Nutmeg and cloves are gathered in the Moluccas, cinnamon in Ceylon. Yet these wonderlands of exotic commodities also provoke a more anxious metaphysical speculation. Off Mozambique, Vasco comes upon some unknown islands with waves frothing on their beaches. He decides to ignore them, but has to pause when the islanders sail out to the visiting fleet. The meeting compels the Europeans to think relativistically: islands are heterodox worlds where foreign gods are worshipped, so their very existence is a lesson in comparative religion. The Sheik in whose domain the Portuguese have trespassed insists on examining the books that codify their belief; he suspects they are Turks. Near Mombasa, Vasco hears enticing reports of an island where Christians and Muslims peacefully coexist. Such stories are plausible because this expansive, elasticized world is a poetic fiction. Camões rearranges the globe and adjusts its moral equilibrium, managing in the process to settle a dispute between the austere Christian God and the capricious divinities of Olympus. Venus favours Vasco, and redirects the winds to keep him on course; Mars and Neptune, who persecute Odysseus, also defer to the Portuguese. Only Bacchus holds out, resenting the encroachment on India, his power base. Camões disposes of the problem by cheerfully admitting that these celestial patrons are merely a troop of dead metaphors; the classical gods go into exile in the vacancy east of Africa, leaving the other hemisphere to their biblical successor.

Camões links his own privileged, imperious art with the inventiveness of the mapmakers, who might have fabricated the new worlds they so exactly outline. At the end of the poem, Vasco is granted a prophetic vision. The nymph Tethys tells him about remoter regions like China, which will only be reached by those who come after him. Alluding to Japan, she blames the sea for jealously keeping such places secret; islands like these deserve to be made known, because they show nature at its most self-glorifying. In the original text, the verb she uses is 'afamar-se': nature is staking its claim to fame, publicizing its creative abundance. Fame was the goal of Renaissance heroes, and of Renaissance artists like Camões, a veteran of naval battles and shipwrecks who was a poet only in his spare time. He compliments nature for sharing his ambition. The land's contours are slowly altered by time – Sumatra, Tethys reveals, was once joined to the mainland, and only became an island after the remorseless gnawing of erosion – but the imagination achieves the same result more speedily. For the most part, *The Lusíads* concentrates on tabulating actual islands, but it concludes by inventing an island that appears on no map, conjured up by Venus so that Vasco and his weary, sexually famished crew can enjoy a voluptuous spell of rest and relief. Camões knowingly insists that the goddess has many such outlying possessions, which supplement her home ground of Cythera. But if the island of love already exists, why does he imagine her enticing it from beneath the water? And if its origins are in the depths, why does it hover above the surface like Delos? These are the mysteries of creativity: art is a private island, dedicated to the fulfilment of wishes that are in one way or another piningly erotic.

Unlike Homer's Calypso, Venus does not entrap and impede the onward-bound hero. The sensual idyll is his reward at the end of the journey. Camões first titillates us by describing an orgy, then interprets the revels allegorically.

The nymphs who offer themselves so flagrantly are symbols, he claims, of the honour that is due to the sailors; Venus, born of the spermatic foam that flecked the waves around Cythera, is encouraging the Portuguese to consummate their love affair with the sea. Lamenting the decay of agriculture in Virginia, the *True Declaration* insisted that colonists ought to be 'Stewards of fertilitie' and rebuked the settlers for forgetting that there can be no 'increase without manuring'. The trickling streams, sighing winds and softly ripening fruits described by Camões make this emphasis on mulch and muck seem coarse, but all such islands were laboratories devoted to propagation, either sexual or economic. In 1688 in *The Isle of Pines*, Henry Neville chronicled the fecundity of a castaway called George Pine, wrecked on a warm, amenable island where leisure frees him to spend his time copulating. With the help of four wives, the bounteous paterfamilias begets forty-seven children. By the age of sixty he has totted up 560 descendants 'of both sorts', and at the time of his death can boast of no fewer than 1,789 Pines 'proceeding from his loins' – a family or a plantation? He conjectures that his island, with 'the culture that skilful people might bestow on it, would prove a paradise'. His own contribution is biological rather than cultural: God after all commanded the creatures in Eden to procreate.

Islands like this, where fantasy has free reign, are too good to be true. Cervantes in *Don Quixote* reduces the idyll to a practical joke when the sarcastic Duke awards the goatherd Sancho Panza a non-existent island to govern. The island on which Venus entertains Vasco lies beyond the perimeter of probability, and is precious because it incites us to dream. But Sancho's island exposes the limitations of our perception; he is gulled because he never takes the precaution of establishing whether it has water around it. He is duped into believing that he has ridden to his island on a flying horse, and when he peeps out from behind his blindfold he sees sooty specks – fragments of the firecrackers with which his wooden mount is stuffed – that could be small worlds, negligible planets scattered in space. What use is it to have absolute power on one of these fugitive specks? The Duke reassures him that his island is securely tethered to the abyss, not blown about by the winds, and vouches for its Atlantis-like geometrical layout: it is 'right and straight, round and well-proportioned', as well as being 'fertile and fruitful', like Pine's seraglio. Colonized islands are meant to be cultivated, because their purpose is to prosper. Sancho's island – actually a starveling village marooned on dry land – derides that greed for gain. Its name is Barataria, which means that it is cheap, valueless. Cervantes introduces his account of Sancho's government with a puffed-up apostrophe to the sun, saluted as the 'perpetual discoverer of the Antipodes!' The flourish demeans the strenuous saga of exploration, since from this height discovery is a banal, diurnal occurrence; our volatile, anchorless globe is as insignificant as the fragmentary firecracker glimpsed by Sancho.

He initially scoffs at the idea of an island, so minuscule and trivial, and asks the Duke to award him sovereignty instead over a portion of the infinite sky. He is right to be suspicious, because islands are exceptions to the norm, where our complacent assumptions about human nature may be upset. The Portuguese in *The Lusiads* pause at a speck of land that they take to be one more island. Actually they have stepped onto the west coast of Africa, just above the Cape, and are astonished to see a race of domesticated black men. One of the party accompanies the natives into the bush, wanting to learn – as Camões says – how they treat the earth. But cultural relativism goes only so far, and the encounter ends bloodily, with the hostile blacks reclassified as brutes. Sancho's so-called island compels him to make some hasty, uncomfortable adjustments of his own. It turns out to be a realm of whimsy, with bizarre and tormenting dietary rules. Fat feasts are laid before him, then whisked away while he salivates; the presiding doctor palms him off with a dry wafer, insisting that this is the medicinal regime enforced for governors of Barataria. Although Sancho goes hungry, he learns to be tolerant and governs both justly and wittily. His legislative record does him credit: among other achievements, he penalizes beggars who decorate their bodies with cosmetic sores, lowers the price of shoes, and relaxes restrictions on importing wine. Perhaps it is better to concentrate on local problems rather than seeking to rectify the whole unworthy world, which is Don Quixote's aim. Islands encourage short views, but if a society is small enough it stands a chance of working well. Barataria may be a shoddy, discount-priced substitute for an island, but for a while Sancho turns it into Utopia.

Shakespeare's Antony is wrong to dispense with realms and islands so carelessly. Shakespeare himself apparently never left his native island, and the images he employed when picturing it, as if from high in the air – a precious stone set in a silver sea, a swan's nest afloat on a pool, or Neptune's park, endowed with a 'natural bravery' by its armature of cliffs and choppy seas – suggest that he valued its separateness and singularity. Even so, Imogen in *Cymbeline* reminds her friend Pisanio to 'think/ There's livers out of Britain'. The island that is her home, she adds, does not monopolize the sun; she is on the periphery of a baffling but invitingly wide world, and calculates that she may be safer if she assumes a new identity elsewhere. Pisanio is glad that her imagination can encompass the alarming, bewildering concept of what he calls 'other place'.

That other place is blank, like a stage before it is temporarily peopled and furnished. In dreaming of it, you design it. As in the forest of Arden, how it looks (idyllic or menacing? Ethereal or earthy?) depends on the way you like it; what happens there derives from the private drama of escape or solipsistic retreat you are acting out. Prospero's island in *The Tempest*, floating somewhere between Tunis and Bermuda, is an anatomy of all such fanciful settings – a synonym for imagining, and for the act of projection we perform when we metaphorically transport ourselves elsewhere. The beings that populate it are the products of theatrical feigning, classifiable as monsters because they do not belong to the fleshly, lumpish family of man. The dancing spirits that execute Prospero's commands are likened by one of the courtiers to the unicorn or the phoenix. Another mystified observer notes their 'monstrous shape', yet marvels at their kindness; this does not mean that he considers them to be kin, because they are not 'of/ Our human generation'. He succinctly but circularly defines them as 'islanders, – / For, certes, these are people of the island'. Of the island, not of the earth: they could be extraterrestrials.

Every character in *The Tempest* looks at the island subjectively. Rather than seeing it steadily and as a whole, they see the place partially and unreliably, like Caliban who accuses Prospero of fastening him to 'this hard rock, whiles you do keep from me/ The rest o' th' island'. Ferdinand, equally confined, rejoices in his incarceration. The cell of the lonely mind is the best place for conjuring up visions, which means admiring Miranda. As he says,

> Might I but through my prison once a day
> Behold this maid: all corners else o' the earth
> Let liberty make use of; space enough
> Have I in such a prison.

He has stated a vocational rule: an artist can happily stay in an enclosed room or on a desert island, where the rest of the world can be imagined. Prospero, supposedly dead, explains his resurrection by claiming that 'some subtleties o' the isle...will not let you/ Believe things certain'. Certainty here gives way to conjecture or fanciful supposition. The old councillor Gonzalo remarks on the island's green grass; Antonio insists that it is tawny, tanned by the sun. Ariel first says that he becalmed the wrecked ship in an odd angle of the coast, then refers to this impromptu harbour as a deep nook. Angle is geometrical, suggesting the 'sterile and rock-hard' coast to which Ceres alludes in

Prospero's masque, while nook evokes domestic shelter, like the inglenook of a fireplace. Picture it as you like it. For Caliban, 'the isle is full of noises'. Those noises, like verbal images, momentarily persuade us that they have a visual dimension. But the vistas are illusory: the music makes Caliban think of clouds that open to rain riches on him, though the marvel, he admits, remains invisible. Exhausted by traipsing along paths that sometimes run straight and then pointlessly meander, Gonzalo likens the terrain to a maze: an artificial labyrinth, legible – like Shakespeare's aerial glimpses of islands as swans' nests or inset jewels – only from above.

Shakespeare lived in a time of geographical flux and cartographic profusion. Malvolio in *Twelfth Night*, wrinkling his features into an exaggerated leer, shows off 'more lines than is in the new map with the augmentation of Indies'; the Welsh patriot Fluellen in *Henry V* appeals to 'maps of the world' in the hope that, somewhere in this jabbering plurality, there will be evidence that Macedon is the same place as Monmouth. Charts are as mutable as Malvolio's rubbery face, which is why Fluellen can get away with fondly universalizing his principality. In *The Tempest* too, the stage is a world with an adjustable equator. Ariel rigs up a clothesline hung with gaudy apparel to distract Caliban and the clowns. Being sailors, Stephano and Trinculo refer to it as an equinoctial line, which is tweaked and flexed by their puns. A jerkin that hangs under the line is likely, Stephano suggests, to lose its hair, like a traveller whose head is shorn to mark the rite of passage between hemispheres. Trinculo adds 'We steal by line and level', which further warps a line that – despite its function as the border between upper and lower worlds, meant to debar trespassers like Dante's Ulysses – is merely a notion, vainly imprinted on water.

At the end of the play, Prospero begs not to be left behind on 'this bare island'. But it is only bare or barren because he is weary; it has contracted to a bleak cell where the ego is disconsolately cornered. Earlier – after Caliban showed him 'every fertile inch' of the place and pointed out 'the qualities o' th' isle', distinguishing between springs of fresh water and brine pits – he had reason to be grateful for its abundance. Caliban promises to gather food for the clowns: fish and monkeys, nuts, berries and eggs from a jay's nest. The menu is tantalizingly specific, though it may be as unnutritious as the banquet that vanishes before the courtiers can eat. The colonizing mind prefers to treat the world as a clean slate, erasing whatever already exists. Gonzalo muses about how he might go about reinstating the golden age, if only he had 'plantation of this isle'. He means planning, since nothing needs to be planted – although Antonio and Sebastian cynically remark that he would sow the ground with docks or nettles. Gonzalo's paradise dispenses with agriculture because the plentiful earth needs no help from human 'sweat or endeavour'. He therefore suggests rescinding cultivation and its iniquitous property rights: 'Bourn, bound of land, tilth, vineyard, none;/ No use of metal, corn, or wine, or oil'. But so many negatives make the island unimaginable. Prospero strips it naked, and Gonzalo wipes it clean of the human history that has sullied it. Either way, it is a nowhere, perfect because featureless.

At least Gonzalo values it and guards the idea of the good place. His attitude is the opposite of Antony's: Sebastian sneers that Gonzalo will 'carry this island home in his pocket'. Securely bedded in that pocket, rather than slipping out like Antony's unregarded coins, it preserves its freshness and its power to sustain us: reaching home, Gonzalo will 'give it his son for an apple'. Antonio adds that he will probably sow 'the kernels of it in the sea' to 'bring forth more islands'. The metaphors, despite their mocking intention, enrich reality as islands do. Instead of dribbling to the ground like derisory pennies, the core unfurls roots that grow in water not in earth. When Shakespeare thinks of an island, worlds proliferate as fecklessly as seeds.

Can any island ever be stranger than fiction? We keep our fantasies on file, awaiting the arrival of some new, outlandish discovery to which we can apply them.

Robert Louis Stevenson, who crisscrossed the Pacific in the late 1880s, saw tropical islands as unashamedly pagan versions of those visited by crusaders in medieval romances. He compared the Marquesas to 'the isles of Vivien', the enchantress who was Merlin's rival; an exiled Samoan chieftain reminded him of King Arthur after his last battle, pining for the legendary island of Avalon where his wounds might be healed. The modern knight, sailing in a yacht like the one Stevenson chartered in San Francisco rather than riding on a horse, was a successor to Quixote and other errant idealists. Stevenson's Pacific voyaging reminded him particularly of the twelfth-century Provençal troubadour and prince Jaufré Rudel, who fell in love at a distance with the reputedly beautiful Countess of Tripoli and voyaged across the Mediterranean to find her. Jaufré reached the African coast in time to expire in the arms of his muse, which for Stevenson was the most refined of consummations. In his own case, the desired person became a place, also attainable only in extremis: he died in Samoa in 1894.

Stevenson wandered indefinitely, perhaps aware that to arrive at the blessed island meant death. Sometimes, however, it was the islands that did the wandering. In 1841 Herman Melville, sailing on the whaling boat *Acushnet*, put in at the Galápagos Islands. The twenty-five clumps of blackened volcanic ash were then known as the Encantadas. Their reputation for enchantment had less to do with their quaint fauna – what Darwin six years earlier called 'insulated species', like the gargantuan tortoises on which he piggy-backed during his stopover – than with their vagrancy. Naval charts disagreed about where to position them. The Pacific was a limbo around which such gobbets of land could migrate: the *Bounty* mutineers chose to hide on Pitcairn because it too had fallen into a crevice between divergent maps. A similar group of wandering islands – a symptom of instability for the map-making sixteenth century – appears in Edmund Spenser's allegory *The Faerie Queene*. The ferryman who is the hero's stern guide complains that they 'to and fro do ronne/ In the wide waters', and advises Guyon to sail past. Not even a reminiscence of the sacred island that migrated around the Aegean can make amends for these 'stragling plots': Spenser, adding a commercial reproof to moral disapproval, remarks that Delos before Jupiter anchored it 'ne made for shipping any certaine port'. What good is an island if it does not supply a berth for traders, and a base for the gunboats that protect them?

When Melville published a set of meditations on the Enchanted Isles in 1854, he gave some of the sketches epigraphs from *The Faerie Queene*. The ferryman's denunciation introduces Melville's view of the islands as piles of cinders dumped in a vacant lot. They were no longer places of moral peril, even though Melville warned that the winds around them were 'unreliable'; instead they were abysmal, reversing evolution in a habitat fit only for reptiles – lizards, snakes and iguanas – which all express themselves in a symphonically sibilant hiss. Spenser's islands harbour 'dreadfull pourtraicts of deformitee', rejected by Dame Nature, who is the mother of us all. But the pilgrim advises Guyon not to be afraid: the 'fearful shapes' are illusory, and they vanish when the virtuous man raises his staff. The overgrown, apparently immortal Galápagos tortoises, so stupidly stubborn as they crawled across the deck of Melville's ship, looked to him like victims of a 'diabolical enchanter', and he had no faith in an easy exorcism. He was troubled by the abortive malpractice or malfeasance of nature, which had hidden away its experimental failures in this remote recess of the ocean. Penguins alarmed him, since being 'neither fish, flesh, nor fowl' they could be assigned to none of the conventional taxonomic categories; pelicans appeared to be doing a solemn, morbidly motionless penance for some obscure crime. The islands were an underworld, a charred inferno that dredged up the messy chaos of our origins.

Melville's visit to this enchanted or bewitched place inevitably made him remember *The Tempest*, although now Caliban not Prospero was its presiding spirit. The sketches conclude with the tale of the rancorous hermit Oberlus, based on a marooned Irishman who holed up on Hood's Isle where he trapped, enslaved and abused passing sailors. Melville imagines him muttering Caliban's claim, 'This island's mine by Sycorax my mother'. But this ignoble savage has not inherited his grim domain; he is a stranger here, having jumped ship. Perhaps the quotation implies that Oberlus – blistered by exposure to the sun, besmirched by the earth, shaggily hirsute and unkempt – is the personification of the place, 'a volcanic creature thrown up by the same convulsion which exploded into sight the isle', akin to the iguanas that scuttled over it. Melville points out that Juan Fernández, on which the self-ostracized Selkirk spent his grumpy exile, is in the vicinity of the Galápagos. Islands are no longer diagrams of a perfect society like Atlantis or Utopia; they suit antisocial ingrates who possess a 'scorn for all the rest of the universe'. The story ends with Melville encouraging a pious contempt for the immured Oberlus, 'since it is philanthropy to hate a misanthrope'. How in this location can we uphold the fond ideal of the human family?

Thanks to Stevenson, Prospero's white magic regained control of the South Seas. Sailing towards the Paumoto Islands on that first voyage from San Francisco, he felt he was travelling through 'a new province of creation…sown with islands', as if Gonzalo's scattered seeds had budded like polyps. Stevenson watched the sandy clumps emerge from the opalescent haze and melt back into it, and recalled Prospero's description of the theatrical show he both created and destroyed: 'Islands we beheld in plenty, but they were of "such stuff as dreams are made on", and vanished at a wink, only to reappear in other places'. The islands, like works of art, are mirages – products of an optical sorcery that cannot be content with our skimpy reality.

2. 'ONE. ME. ALONE.'

Donne was wrong to say that no man is an island: every man inhabits one. The 1624 *Meditation* in which Donne makes his assertion ends by sonorously insisting that we need not ask for whom the bell tolls, because – thanks to our fraternal connection with our fellow beings – any death counts as a personal loss. Such a flush of benevolence makes us feel better about ourselves, but Donne exaggerates when he contends that a clod washed away by the sea lessens Europe or argues that each of us feels impoverished if the ocean engulfs the manor of a friend. A continent hardly misses a handful of soil; in the case of the friend's calamity, most of us would secretly, shame-fully congratulate ourselves that our own property was intact before we began to feel altruistic. In principle we are 'involved in mankind', but in practice we remain instinctively selfish, as Donne knew only too well. His finest poems are about the cerebral disparity of men and women who struggle to be united for a tenuous, sticky moment as their bodies make love. Islands worried him because of their obstinate, unruly individuality; he thought of them as asymmetrical growths that mar God's well-proportioned universe, and in *The First Anniversary* he suggests that Tenerife rears so high that it seems likely to shipwreck the moon as it cruises past. Milton went further, and actually demonized islands. In *Paradise Lost* he likens the baleful bulk of Satan to Tenerife, and compares him as well to a navigable island that is actually – as an unwary sailor discovers when he tries to cast anchor – the scaly back of a whale. Milton notes that another of his fallen angels, Mulciber, supposedly tumbled onto an Aegean island when he was flung out of heaven. The legend refers to the punishment Zeus imposed on Hephaestus, who after plummeting through the sky burrowed into the earth and stoked the volcanic fires that agitate Lemnos. In Milton's cosmography, islands are infernos.

Islands were originally blessed by myth: why should they have become a synonym for perdition? The change occurred because islands, like devils, chose separation; to desert a continent – if you look at the world in this way – is tantamount to denying God. Mankind, collectively created by God in his own image, belongs on the mainland, which has room for our species to do its appointed work of increasing and multiplying. But a man alone on an island finds it hard to accept this version of his origins. In the absence of other creatures or of any creator, he can only assume that he created himself. He lives in the first person singular; the modicum of land he occupies is the ego's allotment. He may complain about his abandonment, yet his situation also gives him grounds for pride. Like Belial in *Paradise Lost*, he accepts hellish pain as the price he must pay for 'this intellectual being'.

In the seventeenth century Descartes formulated a new existential rule – 'Cogito ergo sum' – and in so doing expelled God from the island that is the individual's exclusive realm. Henceforth, this cramped place was to be the symbol of our existential predicament. After his shipwreck, Robinson Crusoe takes stock of his situation. 'I am singl'd out and separated, as it were, from all the World to be miserable,' he writes in his journal. He adds a paraphrase, finding more ways to say the same intolerable thing: 'I am divided from mankind, a solitaire, one banished from humane society'. You don't have to be marooned to feel this way. The island is optional – or it is, perhaps, the self-generating Cartesian mind. Reimagined by Defoe, the extreme, unlikely experience of one disgruntled sailor became a fable exploring our eternal solitude.

In 1704 the cantankerous buccaneer Alexander Selkirk quarrelled with his captain and demanded to be put ashore on the rugged island of Juan Fernández, six hundred miles south of Valparaiso; he spent a little over four years there before a passing ship took him home. He retreated to his home-town in Fife where he lived as a morose, drunken recluse, preferring a cave to his parents' house. The essayist Richard Steele met Selkirk after his return, and remarked that his experience was unique in human history. The judgment may seem exaggerated, but it is the truth. Selkirk's experience forced him to confront his fragile isolation, and when Defoe opened up his mind in *Robinson Crusoe* he became an exemplary modern man – the individual disconnected from family and community and powered by an obstinate, acquisitive will; the lone subject in a world of obtuse material objects. On this island, what we call the self came into being. No such setting had ever been imagined before. Atlantis or Utopia were convivial places, able to accommodate entire cities or cultures. Selkirk's rocky island, with its volcanic peaks and forested ravines, was a cage designed for a prisoner in solitary confinement, and before long it closed in on him. The turtles he ate made his bowels boil. At night while he slept, rats nipped at his feet and nibbled his clothes. It horrified him to think that when he died they would make a meal of his remains. Though not especially pious, he recited the Bible out loud to ensure that he retained the power of speech; even so, his rescuers found him to be incoherent, mumbling and mashing words. They also suspected that he had cheered himself up by sexually consorting with the nanny goats that were his companions. What happened on Selkirk's island haunted the urbane, enlightened eighteenth century. Could civility and even humanity be so easily revoked or discarded?

Steele spared his readers by telling a softened version of the story. He conceded that life on his own so depressed Selkirk that for a while he considered suicide; yet according to Steele's account, Selkirk steadfastly indoctrinated himself with scripture, applied his 'force of reason' to the study of navigation, and after eighteen months was 'thoroughly reconciled' to his situation. Sadder, wiser minds doubted that such an experience could ever be psychologically bearable. Samuel Johnson, chilled by his visit to the Hebrides, regarded islands as alien places, unfit for our species. In 1771 he mocked British efforts to conquer the Falkland Islands, whose 'bleak and gloomy solitude' was 'thrown aside from human use'.

Edward Cooke, a ship's captain who published a narrative of his voyage to the South Seas in 1712, remarked on the tedium of Selkirk's sojourn but skimped on detail because he considered the castaway's experience to be 'barren', as starkly boring as his island. Cooke believed that our species is 'naturally fond of novelty', which would seem to disqualify Selkirk as a subject for literary treatment. Minna in Scott's *The Pirate* yawns when Cleveland summarizes his solitary month on one of the keys in the West Indies, and calls it 'a tale of nothing'. But Defoe, as ingenious as his hero, wrote his novel in the absence of novelty. He could dispense with newness – the incidents and adventures that Cooke expected – because he paid such close attention to daily happenings, the cycle of chores and routines that constitute existence for most people, whether they live on desert islands or not. Defoe's boldest decision was to lengthen his hero's term of trial. Crusoe is stranded on the island for twenty-seven years. Considering that Selkirk began to founder linguistically in a fraction of this time, the elongation threatens to stretch probability – except that Nelson Mandela spent just as many years in prison on Robben Island outside Cape Town, and left with his mind and his moral sense intact. Defoe further handicapped Crusoe by depriving him of Selkirk's few advantages. Selkirk occupied a ramshackle beach hut made from planks, canvas and rushes by previous castaways. Crusoe gets no such helping hand. He fabricates his own shelter, and goes on to construct an entire estate, with a town house and a country retreat, annexes for storing goods, and a fortified wall to keep out imaginary burglars. Necessity makes him an inventor; his ingenuity is backed up by a heroic capacity for work and a noble refusal to accept defeat. He cannot rely, like Prospero, on the labour-saving abracadabra of magic. Only the savages, frightened away by gunfire, believe that his island is 'enchanted'. A few years after writing the novel, Defoe visited the denuded, demythologized north of Scotland. Geographers, he said, found it hard to describe such featureless territory, so they filled it 'with hills and mountains, as they do the inner parts of Africa with lions and elephants, for want of knowing what else to place there'. The remark underlines his honesty in refusing to infest Crusoe's island with spurious marvels. He discounted stories about the dangerous waters around Stroma, an island between the mainland and the Orkneys, because to repeat such superstitions would be like claiming that witches haunted the place. Defoe does not permit islands to be hideouts for unemployed gods or frisky malevolent spirits. Their very emptiness is what makes them elemental: a proving ground for physical or spiritual endurance, as bare as a sporting arena or a monastic cell. Rather than merely surviving his ordeal, Crusoe triumphs over it – and although he complains of his miserable loneliness, his victory belongs to all mankind, because the uncooperativeness of nature has, in the course of our history, been broken down by the dogged persistence and the momentary inspirations of minds like his. Cast out of comfortable paradise, we were abandoned in a hostile world; after aeons, we made it a home. Crusoe re-enacts that epochal achievement in less than three decades.

At first, like a baleful allegorist who imprints occult meanings on nature, Crusoe decides to call his 'dismal unfortunate island...the Island of Despair'. A few years later, hustled out to sea by a furious current during a journey of circumnavigation, he stares back at his 'desolate solitary island', which has now become 'the most pleasant place in the world'. He addresses endearments to it in the hope of a reunion: he now calls it 'my beloved island' and in a lovelorn lament says 'O happy desert…I shall never see thee more'. For all our accomplishments, we are an ingrate species. No sooner have we domesticated wildness than we become impatient to leave our haven. By the time we look back at the home we have spurned, it may be too late to return. Anxious to ascertain whether he is 'on the continent or on an Island', Crusoe climbs to the top of a hill and sees that he is 'environ'd every way with the sea'. The sight dismays him, but before he long he is proud to confirm this separateness. 'I had a great mind to see the whole island', he announces before he trudges round its circumference, as if his greatness of mind were commensurate with his ability to 'keep all the island…in my view'. Later he sails round it in his homemade boat. On a clear day he can see over the strait to 'the Main, or Continent of America'. Friday longs to cross the water, but Crusoe – solipsistically dividing the self from the rest of the inert but inimical world, unwilling to be 'a piece of the continent, a part of the main' as Donne put it – says there is good reason to be glad about this ostracism. What would happen if Friday rejoined his people? '"Why then," said I to him, "They will kill you."'

The British Isles, for Defoe, were an extension of Crusoe's little kingdom. Inside its trench of water, the amalgamated nation guarded its political integrity and its quaint, quirky oddity. Defoe boasted that it took the Roman general Agricola seven campaigns to subdue Britain, which demonstrated the advantage of insularity. During the 1720s he followed Crusoe's example on a national scale and made a series of looping trips from northern Scotland to Cornwall, following coastal roads and symbolically setting foot in the sea at the points where land ran out at the eastern, western, northern and southern extremities of the country. In *A Tour Around the Whole Island of Great Britain* he appraised the island as a synonym for wholeness and an impregnable storehouse. True, he scoffed at the Isles of Scilly as 'excrescences', too small and rocky to be profitable. But geologically he appraised the mainland as 'one solid rock…formed by Nature to resist the otherwise irresistible power of the ocean' – and of course to baffle invaders. In the far southwest, deposits of tin and copper enriched this fence of barbed stone: Britain's rampart was a hoard of valuable metals, converting to cash Shakespeare's image of the island as 'a precious stone set in a silver sea'. Defoe concluded the first part of his *Tour* when he reached Land's End, which he took to be a last, definitive full stop. This was where 'Nature ended her account, when she meted out the island, and where she fixed the utmost western bounds of Britain'. An account is both a tale and a tally, at once artful and calculating. Defoe admires Nature as a storyteller who is also a scrupulous bookkeeper: the land apportioned to Britain is just enough for the establishment of a unified, efficient, productive commonwealth.

Crusoe creates internal islands within the margins of the larger one. He pitches a tent on a semicircle of flat ground on a hill, stakes out a fence, then drags all his provisions, ammunition and stores into the stockade. He makes a second aedicular enclosure by doubling the tent to keep out the rain, and the umbrella he fabricates from the skin of animals serves him as an extra ambulatory shelter: it drains off downpours, as he says, like a 'penthouse'. Other enclosures contain his cattle and his cornfields. Eventually he adds extra fortifications to make the outer wall ten feet thick. The unmanned muskets and pistols that he rigs to the bastion, like gun emplacements on the coast, provide him with a troop of invisible guards. This is his little England; it is also the ego's embattled castle. Ensconced there, his imperative is to keep intruders out. Crusoe's survival depends on his aptitude at killing: Cartesian man must rid the world of competitors. When he is washed up on the island, his first thought is that he has 'no weapon either to hunt or kill any creature'. Eventually he retrieves a gun from the wreck, and shoots a bird. The concussion announces the advance of civilization, like the sound of an axe in a forest, and Crusoe assumes that his is 'the first gun that had been fir'd there since the creation of the world'. He is now the creator, with the right to eliminate any creature he considers expendable. When Luis Buñuel filmed *Robinson Crusoe* in Mexico in 1954 he squeamishly took care to disarm the hero. Famished, Buñuel's character raids a bird's nest, and finds a chick hatching from an egg. He removes the top half of the shell, like a man settling down to tackle a boiled egg at breakfast. The sight of the timid fledgeling changes his mind, and he tenderly replaces the cracked shell. It is a charming moment, but quite uncharacteristic of Defoe's hero, who massacres birds without even knowing whether they are edible.

Earlier islands were places of sensual leisure. George Pine, explaining his excessive production of heirs, blames his island, where 'idleness and a fullness of everything begot in me a desire for enjoying the women'. Crusoe, however, keeps relentlessly and perhaps pointlessly busy. Cut off from what he calls 'humane commerce', he cannot contribute to an economy because there is no one with whom he can exchange goods or engage in barter. The money he salvages from the wrecked ship is, as he admits with a grimace, worthless on a desert island. But his circumstances favour work of a different kind, which assesses value differently and is as much concerned with pleasure as with utility: we call it art. The industrious Crusoe is also an artificer, who bends twigs into a basket and moulds lumps of clay into pots. He calls his jars 'ugly', but his frustration demonstrates that he has a notion of beauty. Art probably began with such murky dabblings, which go back to the infancy of the race and to the individual's earliest play: Crusoe likens his crude pottery to a child's mud pies. Although Crusoe is often taken to be a dull materialist, Defoe's vocabulary stretches across the gap between the commercial and the aesthetic. Crusoe's 'magazine', for instance, is the improvised warehouse in which he hoards his kit – 'the biggest', he believes, 'ever...laid up...for one man', as if he were the proprietor of a department store and its sole customer.

But a magazine is also a compendium of writings, one of the journalistic innovations of Defoe's period. Crusoe extends the meaning of such words, as when he wittily calls his menagerie of goats 'a living magazine of flesh, milk, butter and cheese'. Magazines of the literary kind are closer to Crusoe's livestock than to his cupboards of dead commodities: people buy them to have contact with the thoughts and feelings of writers, which are valuable even though they cannot be consumed or used in any practical sense (except perhaps as wrapping paper for other commodities).

The island is a study as well as a workshop, and Crusoe overcomes the privation of solitude and the monotony of duration by writing. This is his conversation with himself and his competition with time. By differentiating the days as they pass, he organizes them into a narrative, with himself as its invincible hero. He determines 'to minute down the days of the month on which any remarkable thing happen'd to me, and first by casting up times past'. He minutes his life like a secretary taking notes at a meeting, though his diminishing supply of ink – which he dilutes 'till it was so pale it scarce left any appearance of black upon the paper' – requires him to be selective about minutiae. He cannot help admitting that the elongation of his term is an agony, as the small words that stand for temporal units yawningly dilate. Thus he reports that his dutiful reflections 'took me up many hours, days; nay, I may say, weeks or months'. That summary is easily written; it was surely not so easy to live through such an endless period of self-mortification. Only after 'some years' does he manage to teach his parrot to speak. The repetitive drill must have been maddening, but the written record abbreviates it in a briskly triumphant sentence. Keeping a journal, Crusoe frames a day at a time and tabulates its achievements. But to hold a pen is a reflective act, and it withdraws the writer from the instantaneous, successive medium in which we live; the moment is already past when we record it, which is why we value art's capacity for representation – for reviving and reinterpreting the lapsed present. Crusoe is compiling an archive, not scribbling a daily newspaper. Hence his meditations on coincidence and the recurrence of significant dates, like 30 September – his birthday, and also the date of his shipwreck, which he comes to see as a second birth, a miraculous salvation. The literary discipline of retrospection brings him to a belated, contented understanding. No wonder that it is such a tragedy for him to run out of ink (which, despite his expertise in other areas, he never learns to make). The fluid is as precious as blood, and his faded, watery texts look anaemic. But by the time all the ink is used up, the habit of looking backwards and inwards has become second nature. He now behaves like a writer, whether or not he is able to write. The island – by imposing silence and sedentariness on him, and training him to think about life as well as living it – has taught him how to be an artist.

Aloneness is no longer an infliction: like a novelist or a dramatist, Crusoe multiplies the single self into a company of divergent, occasionally quarrelsome characters. When he deliberates about unloading the wrecked ship, he summons 'a council, that is to say, in my thoughts', as if he had a parliamentary debating chamber, noisy with dissenting voices, inside his head. His creatures answer him back, or at least acknowledge him as their creator. At one point he has two parrots, which antiphonally address him as Robin Crusoe; as when he calls that psychological council, the doubling of voices recognizes his own duality. He is complete in himself without a sexual partner, and the usual interdependence of man and woman has been replaced by the complementarity of man and implement. Before leaving the island he arms Friday and the Spanish sailor, who stay behind to prosecute his war against the savages. He hands over muskets with a supply of powder and bullets, 'charging them to be very good husbands of both'. Again a word is used with a cunningly ambiguous awareness of its history. Husbandry first meant the careful cultivation of the land, and when the word extended to cover marriage it ranked a spouse among the householder's chattels or defined the man as the woman's provider. Crusoe omits the wife, or replaces her with a weapon. His successors have advanced beyond tilling the soil; they do their cultivating with guns not ploughs.

The ego is a jealous god, and Crusoe accordingly is a strict monotheist. In George Miller's film of the novel, released in 1996, the Crusoe of Pierce Brosnan berates Friday for believing in a crocodile as the creator. Their dispute causes them to break off relations; the split is healed when Crusoe apologizes. Their 'universe of two', he says, should not be broken up by a doctrinal quarrel. Defoe's hero is less tolerant. Catechizing Friday, he asks who made him. Friday misunderstands, and thinks Crusoe wants to know who his father was. Crusoe rephrases the question, asking who made the earth. Friday attributes this to 'one old Benamuckee', about whom he knows nothing except that he is very old. Could he be identifying Crusoe – whose white whiskers he venerates – as this omnipotent elder? A little archly, Crusoe wonders why 'if this old person had made all things...all things [do not] worship him'. Friday responds that 'all things do say O' to Benamuckee, and Crusoe deduces that to say 'O' means to pray. Having named and then enslaved Friday, Crusoe believes that he should enjoy a creator's privileges; perhaps he is nominating himself as worthy of worship, fit to be apostrophized. It is a demand that an artist has the right to make. Caliban sneers at Prospero's pretence of kingship: how can the island be a kingdom if Caliban is his only subject? Prospero outwits him by claiming to be a creator, not just a master. The 'thing of darkness', he explains, is part of him. Defoe's hero deifies himself without having to make such conces-sions. Friday consents to believe in Crusoe's God, which means that he has unquestioning faith in Crusoe. The Cartesian cogitator performs the ultimate mental experiment: he reconstructs the fabric of society, then fills in the supernatural vacancy above it. An empty island is the nucleus for a world we create in our own image.

Donne's assertion that no man is an island is catchy, whether or not it turns out to be true. Ernest Hemingway relied on it as a slogan supporting comradeship and even communism in his novel about the Spanish civil war, *For Whom the Bell Tolls*. But by choosing for his title a later phrase from the meditation, Hemingway shifted the emphasis from our solidarity in life to the egalitarianism of death. In effect he refutes Donne: the novel is about blowing up a bridge, severing a means of connection. Robert Jordan, an American volunteer in the Republican army, chooses to die alone, sending away the woman he loves. Death may equalize us, but we still must confront it as individuals and submit to its scrutiny of our moral worth. The true creed of these characters is incompatible with their teamwork as partisans. Andrés, carrying a message for Jordan, states the principle they live by as he tries to convince some sentries to let him pass. They ask how many combatants there are in his band. He gives a jerky, iterated reply, in three words that refuse to be adulterated by sharing a sentence: 'One. Me. Alone'. When the sentries look sceptical, he says it again, furiously emphatic: 'I AM ALONE'.

For Whom the Bell Tolls is set inland. Jordan comes from Montana, which as one of his Spanish colleagues remarks is presumably mountainous terrain. It is a telling comment: mountains are as unsociable as islands, and El Sordo is enraged when he is ambushed and left wounded on a hill, 'only utilizable as a place to die'. Is the earth ever anything else for a Hemingway character? The novelist found a topography to match his outlook in *Islands in the Stream*, which he was writing at the time of his suicide in 1961. The islands are the Bahamas, in particular Bimini; the stream is the Gulf Stream, which is actually a euphemism, as the hero recognizes. Thomas Hudson – a beachcombing artist who spends most of his time fishing – reflects on the apparent passivity of the water, feminized because of its wallowing, messy depths. 'Why is she so dishonest?' asks Hudson of the ocean. He knows about the unstable temper of rivers, and is aware that 'a stream can be completely friendly'. But an ocean is an inveterate liar, affecting calm before her next spasm of wildness confounds you. Hence its threat to the islands, male monoliths that try to withstand its assault. The female element is liquid, mixed with screaming air: in the novel, Bimini is thrashed by a hurricane. Like Jordan, Hudson has a home in Montana, and in other moods he views the sea as a dried-up mountain range. It is 'broken country', as rugged as the gulches and crevasses of the Badlands in South Dakota, and it offers the same challenge to the man who struggles to keep his balance or stay afloat. Almost paraphrasing Crusoe, the reclusive Hudson says 'I've learned how to live by myself pretty well and I work hard'. But such self-discipline is a counsel of despair; the heroism of Hemingway's men is confirmed by their inevitable defeat. Hudson dies during a wartime skirmish in the vicinity of Guantánamo, and as his consciousness fades he looks at the lagoon of another island which he is 'quite sure, now, he would never paint'. Beaches mark an end to the crumbling earth, and earlier in *Islands in the Stream* the entire world ends on Bimini – or at least it does so prospectively, in an eschatological fantasy which a garrulous bar-tender wants Hudson to paint. In the suggested scenario the ocean boils over, disgorging armadas of carnivorous sharks. The drunken islanders swill down oceans of their own, and use empty rum bottles to batter the devils who cart them away to hell.

Hemingway's ocean engulfs Bimini. But what if we imagine the desiccation of that flailing sea, hardening it into a network of highways, a confluence of streaming metal? J. G. Ballard's *Concrete Island* describes a Crusoe stranded in the middle of a city during the 1970s. As a lesson in survival, Defoe's version of the story is in Ballard's opinion too much like a tropical holiday. A contemporary urban equivalent, as he points out, would be less delightful: think about being stalled in a tunnel on an underground train, or in a jammed elevator halfway up a skyscraper. *Concrete Island* reproduces such predicaments in the open air. An architect is driving home on an elevated section of the Westway leading out of London; one of his tyres has a blow-out, and his car lunges through a crash barrier and skids onto a traffic island, where the exotic landscape familiar from stories about castaways is grubbily duplicated. Coarse, windblown grass tosses 'like the waves of a brisk sea', running into a 'jungle of refuse'. Lanes of traffic skim past feet away, his house is only a few miles off. But an injured leg handicaps him. Tethered to the spot over an aching, delirious weekend, he might as well be abandoned on 'an alien planet', which some non-human race of engineers has furnished with pillars of reinforced concrete. In a few feverish days he races through the progressive mastery of the environment that took Crusoe three decades. He decides to signal for help, and using the burnt rubber guards from his car's spark plugs as 'writing materials' he smears an appeal on the concrete. This skilful adaptation pleases him, even if it produces no result: it proves that he can 'dominate the island'.

Crusoe achieves this dominion with the help of salvage from his wrecked ship, and Ballard's man ransacks his disabled vehicle and recycles its battery of gadgets. 'Was the entire island an extension of the Jaguar?' he asks. The illusion of mastery elicits from him a grand statement, spoken 'like a priest officiating at the eucharist of his own body', which flatly refutes Donne's meditation. The marooned driver totters around the outskirts of his scruffy domain, and as he goes he symbolically sheds bits and pieces of his torn flesh, like Christ donating his body and blood to his followers. He imagines depositing his smashed leg at the crash barrier, his hands on the steel fence that ripped them, his battered chest against a concrete crash barrier. Each stage of the solemn ritual relieves his pain by dehumanizing him: by the time it concludes, he is as insentient as an automobile. He completes the circuit by uttering the sentence which Ballard calls priestly, and says out loud 'I am the island'. This is meant to be his vindication, though perhaps it is his undoing. If he is the island, shouldn't he stay there, rather than fretting about escape? At the end of the novel, he hides from potential rescuers, and happily scavenges edible scraps from the perimeter of his sovereign domain. Steele thought Selkirk's case was unique; as Ballard's fable implies, it is now common, even banal. We are all self-enclosed, retentive Crusoes, cut off from the world by our double-glazed windows and (interesting word) insulated lofts, by our burglar alarms or by the electronic cocoon – MP3 player with earphones, hands-free mobile phone – which shields us when we venture into the street. Every city-dweller lives in effect on a solitary island. The ocean is the buffeting crowd of other people, and we exert ourselves to stay dry.

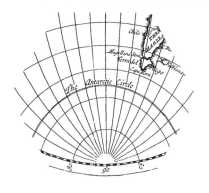

8. CRUSOE AND COMPANY

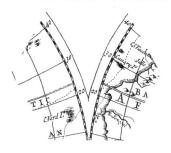

Crusoe's solitude is intolerable, even inconceivable – a rebuff to our notion of ourselves as gregarious animals, and to literature's curiosity about relationships. Other people matter less to him than handy possessions like a pipe or a gun. He carries his insularity back to England where, as he casually remarks, he marries ('not either to my disadvantage or dissatisfaction', he grudgingly adds), begets three children, then uses his wife's death as an excuse to desert his family by shipping off again to the East Indies. In a poem by Elizabeth Bishop, a Crusoe more sedately resettled in England looks back on his island's fifty-two squat, stubby volcanoes, along with its snails, gulls, goats and tortoises, and fondly remembers the offshore waterspouts which teetered in the air like 'sacerdotal beings'. 'Beautiful, yes,' he adds, 'but not much company.' When company arrives in the form of Friday, the Crusoe in Bishop's poem cannot help sneaking a look at his 'pretty body'. Defoe's character reveals no such covert craving; in his lack of empathy, he is scarcely human.

Conceding that Crusoe's situation was not that of 'social man', Rousseau commended him all the same because his example taught children how to cope with a tricky, obstructive world. He could safely be admired so long as his island remained a model of political economy, with no questions asked about the islander's emotional obtuseness. In 1782 in *Letters from an American Farmer*, the French immigrant Hector St John de Crèvecoeur described a society of industrious, cooperative Crusoes on Nantucket, off the Massachusetts coast. The 'ungrateful soil' and patchy grass of the sandy, treeless island serve as a goad to labour; Martha's Vineyard, equally barren, turns out to be a 'nursery' – but of pilots and seamen, who do their best to sow the waves. This, Crèvecoeur argues, is a proper habitat for industrious virtue, since vice requires a more bosomy terrain and a balmier climate. All the same, it lacks a narrative of struggle, either against nature or rampaging savages. The inhabitants of Nantucket have 'no annals, for they are not a race of warriors'. If we didn't fight wars, would we have any need for history? Crèvecoeur dismisses the belligerence of epic and adjusts his writing to the repetitive calm of pastoral. His farmers quietly toil on their individual allocations of 'territorial property' – forty acres as a home lot, a tract of pasture adequate for exactly 560 sheep; the common plantation 'raises a sort of emulation', as the islanders zealously fertilize their assigned strips, like modern suburbanites mowing their lawns and painting their picket fences to impress the neighbours. In this benign view, Crusoe's solipsism and his acquisitive drive are not incompatible with social harmony. Nor is loneliness a state of alienated anguish: Crèvecoeur chooses the far end of the island, with its view out across the ocean, as a spot designed for rumination, complaining only that it lacks a clump of ancient trees 'to shelter contemplation in its beloved solitude'. A Crusoe soothed by such romantic habits is no longer a self-generating ego; he has begun to merge with his surroundings. The children of the Nantucket settlers looked to Crèvecoeur like hybrid creatures, 'ruddy as the cherry, healthy as the fish they lived on, hardy as pine knots' – products of a marriage between man, ocean and forest.

By the end of the eighteenth century, the island had changed from a cell for the ego's solitary confinement to a resort where the querulous mind could relax into nature. Haydn's opera *L'Isola disabitata*, composed in 1779, explores these opposed options by exhibiting two female Crusoes, treacherously abandoned by a man who leaves them to languish on a desert island for thirteen years. Costanza despairs, like Cowper's Selkirk, and spends the time melodiously pondering suicide. But her younger sister Silvia takes a Rousseauesque delight in the unspoiled island and does not miss what she calls 'le delizie europee'. Costanza, too constant by half, is the cultural warrior, even more determined than Crusoe the diarist to make a monument that will outlast and vanquish time. She therefore inscribes her own funerary memorial on a rock with the remains of a sword. Silvia rejoices in her escape from the oppression of custom and civilized morality, and rather than yearning for society she adopts the island's tame livestock as her friends. Why not adapt to the environment, rather than subduing or exploiting it as Crusoe does? Johann David Wyss, an army chaplain, converted Defoe's hero to this new romantic life in *The Swiss Family Robinson*, first published in 1812–13. Wyss's hero is a pastor and a paterfamilias, shipwrecked with his wife and four sons while sailing to New Holland. They spend ten years on their island; when the chance of rescue arrives, the father elects to stay, while sending two of his sons back to Europe.

During their time as castaways, they inevitably consult the Bible and follow its precepts, but their other sacred text is *Robinson Crusoe*, which one of the boys finds stowed at the bottom of a clothes chest. They adopt Crusoe as an honorary ancestor and accept the novel as their 'counsellor', although it is not exactly true, as young Fritz claims, that heaven has destined them to share his fate. Whereas Crusoe was a man alone, they are a family. Indeed they are the holy family, housed in the makeshift equivalent of a manger with their pet animals – dogs, fowls, pigeons, sheep and goats – ranged around them. The father shoulders a gun, but his armed aggression is softened by the 'kind mother'. He performs mechanical miracles, constructing a forge or rigging up a turning-lathe and a loom, while her speciality is domestic nurture. She produces a needle and thread from a bottomless 'enchanted bag' that contains her wonder-working household kit; she plants cotton which she weaves into clothes for her brood, and her husband teasingly remarks that she is often so busy at her spinning wheel that she scarcely has time 'to dress our dinners'. She collects down plucked from birds as padding for these garments, and makes carpets from the pelts of goats. Insulation, thanks to her, acquires another meaning: it comes to mean a protective cladding, an extra layer of warmth. Although they apply their skills to create a facsimile of bourgeois society, they are more inclined than Crusoe to see nature as a provider, not a harsh leveller. The earth even supplies them with soap in the form of fuller's earth, which was used to launder woollens in the days before detergents. One of the sons is surprised when his father identifies this fine, white-ish soil, and says that soap is surely 'the result of human industry': he assumes that cleanliness is a benefit of our civilized state. The father agrees that soap can be expensively and exhaustingly concocted with salt and grease, but why bother? Earth does not only besmirch us; it also supplies a means of cleansing. Crusoe presumably had fewer sanitary scruples, since hygiene is a consequence of our sensitivity to the opinions of others. The younger Swiss boys complain about another divergence from the prototype, and wonder why they have no Man Friday. One of them votes for 'savages, warfare and encounters', but their elder bother Fritz sensibly concludes that they are better off 'without such a companion'. Nature is providentially mild; there is no need to declare war on the idea of wildness, or to capture and control its abject representative.

The flora and fauna of their domain are bizarrely eclectic. One small island contains both strawberries and pineapples. An American tree called the candleberry grows there, as does the Indian fig or prickly pear. Buffaloes consort with kangaroos, and there are sightings of boa constrictors and hyenas. This jumbling of geography may have an ulterior motive. In a Sunday parable, the father describes an island called Earthly Abode, whose inhabitants yearn for promotion to the Heavenly City. His allegory explains the jumbled livestock: the island has rolled back its borders and spread across the oceans to fill up the globe, reuniting the family of man and the more extended, disparate family of beasts. It is a kind of intermediary Atlantis – perhaps better called Pacifica or Indiana, since it mythically distends to fill up the gaps between America, Australia and India, restoring land bridges across which bison, lions, antelopes and marsupials can companionably roam, with Brazilian parrots fluttering overhead. No wonder the book appealed to the radical philosopher William Godwin, the husband of the feminist Mary Wollstonecraft and the father of Mary Shelley, who published the first English translation of *The Swiss Family Robinson* in 1814. For him it must have been less a fantasy than a political tract, envisaging a natural society that could get along without a government.

Being Swiss, the book's characters, like Godwin, are instinctive republicans. They venerate the 'crowned' pineapple, but their true sympathies lie with the finches that 'exist as a republic' with 'one common nest, inhabited at pleasure by all their tribes'. We are a long way from the autocracy of Crusoe: nature, not red in tooth and claw after all, chastens the monadic ego by teaching it the lesson of friendly coexistence. God pervades the landscape that sustains the family, so they can abandon Crusoe's paranoid reclusion. They discover propitious spots beyond their camp, and give them names that are benedictions: an oasis in the savanna is called Green Valley, a rocky enclave watered by the cascades becomes Arcadia. After ten years they feel they have recreated paradise, and the island would have been Eden, says the pastor, 'if we could but have looked upon men, our brothers!' He is forgetting that the garden in Genesis contained only one connubial pair; the offspring of Adam and Eve arrived after their expulsion from Eden. Nevertheless, an obliging romantic deity soon fulfils his wish. They happen upon a female castaway of genteel birth, which means that procreation is now theoretically possible.

Crusoe begins as primitive man, fumbling to master nature. He is thrust back to the beginning of our history, whereas the Swiss family – who add an epilogue to his story – can take advantage of a world that has been craftily subdued by human expertise. The father has no need to invent the techniques that enforce this control; he merely cites precedents, drawing on his universal knowledge as an ethnographer and anthropologist. How do you domesticate a buffalo calf? He recommends adopting 'the method practised in Italy' by putting a ring through its nose. A wild ass is lassooed using 'the Patagonian method'. When threshing grain, the family follows the Italian example rather than the Swiss: they have nothing with which to tie the bundles, so they throw the stalks into a basket like their southern neighbours who, 'naturally averse to labour, never use sheaves, as being too heavy to carry'. Remoter cultures offer solutions to more recondite problems. How can the half-coagulated oil from the head and dorsal bone of a sperm whale be gathered and stored? They use 'a process…employed in India', scooping the 'precious substance' into wet linen sacks. Their culinary options are equally global. Feasting on the head of a wild boar, they prepare it with truffles 'in the Otaheitan manner' and dig a ditch in which to cook it.

The pastor's Christianity gradually expands into a generous, trusting pantheism. His family worships in a church of living rock: vaulted cliffs above a bay serve as 'a temple elevated to the Eternal', with the sea replacing the conventional floor of marble. Their island contains a potential hell, but it turns out to be harmless. The shaft of a salt mine shows off walls of glinting crystal when they toss mortars in; with these playful flares they harrow hell, and by waving a metaphoric wand transform the abyss into 'the palace of a fairy, or an illuminated temple'. Even bad weather delights them by amplifying nature's harmonious orchestra. They treat the downpours of the rainy season as a concert, with thunder as timpani and the keening gales as wind instruments. Half a century later, nature's music quietened into a lullaby that cradled the castaway. In Offenbach's operetta *Robinson Crusoé*, the wandering hero holds a shell to the ear of his fiancée Edwige, so she can hear the sea's irresistible siren song. The ocean – so threatening for Defoe's hero – now mildly resonates inside the body. Crusoé's voyage to the island is summarized by Offenbach in a symphonic prelude. The sea laps in a gently soporific rhythm, and a shimmer of strings suggests light glinting on water. A storm whipped up by blaring brass and rumbling drums soon abates and its last cadence, like a wave unfurling on the beach, deposits Crusoé on the island. He recognizes it at once, though he has never been there: landlocked in England, he visited it in his dreams, and he longs for darkness, which frees him to converse with the shadowy figures he remembers. Defoe's hero is terrified at night, because unconsciousness makes him vulnerable to attack by predators. Crusoé, who knows that in romantic nature there is nothing to fear, eagerly anticipates encounters with snakes, crocodiles and other tropical wonders.

After only six years his English friends arrive to rescue him, and he is tunefully reunited with Edwige. She may be disconcerted to find that Friday is actually a woman shaggily dressed as a man: Offenbach wrote the part for the mezzo-soprano who first performed Bizet's seductive gypsy in *Carmen*. Defoe's Crusoe worked his way through an intimidating, ennobling trial; his namesake in the operetta may have been enjoying an illicit sexual holiday.

Romantic readers too easily overlooked the misanthropy of Crusoe. Because his island was now so welcoming, he could hardly be blamed for taking up residence there. The twentieth century remembered his perversity, and made the island the setting for modern man's philosophical quarrel with nature. It is the school of capitalism and – after Crusoe commandeers Friday – of imperialism, enslaving half of mankind to ensure its control of markets; less obviously, the island also becomes the place where a solitary consciousness withdraws from the all-encompassing life of nature. As Virginia Woolf pointed out, Defoe actually provides an antidote to romanticism. His novel ignores the sublime romantic spectacle of 'man…standing against a background of broken mountains and tumbling oceans with stars flaming in the sky', instead concentrating on 'a plain earthenware pot in the foreground' and persuading us 'to see remote islands and the solitudes of the human soul' contained in that vessel. Infinity is closed off; art reduces grandiose vistas to the individual's partial angle of vision, narrowing the collective ocean to a personal stream of thoughts and impressions. At best, Crusoe's industrious toil is a kind of occupational therapy, like Woolf's own typesetting in the basement of her house in Bloomsbury. 'To dig, to bake, to plant, to build – how serious these simple occupations are,' she reflects in her essay on the book; 'hatchets, scissors, logs, axes – how beautiful these simple objects are.' Crusoe thought first of function not form, and valued tools and blades as weapons rather than admiring their design. But Woolf saw the island as a cerebral place, the white cell of a stranded mind, and the contents of Crusoe's armoury, toolshed and kitchen cabinet were like archaeological relics that told of a time when people still had manual contact with the world.

This retreat into the mind, the most undiscoverable of islands, also happens to Crusoe in Michel Tournier's novel *Friday*, published in 1967. 'The subject,' reasons Tournier's hero, 'is the disqualified object.' Trees or goats or pots exist only if he sees them, which makes him wonder whether they truly exist at all. 'My hand refutes the thing it holds,' he says. You can imagine Woolf dropping the scissors or the pot on which she fastens her shaky grip. Objects are solid, but the subjective self is ghostly, as ethereal as ectoplasm; there can be no commerce between them. The pot breaks on the floor. But the calamity is averted if the utensils are entirely notional: on the island in J. M. Barrie's *Peter Pan*, the lost children – experts in make believe – eat 'a pretend meal…with nothing whatever on the table, not a mug, nor a crust, nor a spoon'. They know better than to complain about deprivation and scarcity, which constrict the domestic economy of real islands; despite their youth, they are a group of abstract artists, who refute the things their hands are not holding. What we once called the real world has expelled us – cast us out or cast us away. Barrie's boys delight in their playful unreality, 'washing dishes they don't have in a non-existent sink and stowing them in a cupboard that isn't there'.

Tournier's Crusoe is less pleased to find himself surrealized. He feels like the 'excrement' of the island; he thinks of himself as an excrescence because his hyperactive mind has been ejected from the irrational, promiscuous swarm of nature. As such worries reveal, he is a philosopher not a practical engineer, and he spends his time on the island – twenty-eight years, slightly longer than the first Crusoe's term – analysing his own predicament. Tournier updates the experience by a few crucial decades: his Crusoe is wrecked in 1759 and offered the chance of rescue (which he, like the Swiss Robinson, rejects) in 1787. This chronological adjustment makes him an honorary romantic, a transcendental idealist who believes, like Kant, that the mind creates the world into which it is born. 'My brain,' as Crusoe says in Elizabeth Bishop's poem, 'bred islands'. But that perception is only possible when he arrives at a sophisticated sense of the distance between subject and object. Tournier's Crusoe begins by regressing to a primitive condition, venturing further back into our pre-human history than Defoe's hero ever goes. He coats himself in mud and merges with the primal mire; later he lubricates his skin with sour milk and squeezes into a uterine cave, curled up inside the body of the island as if refusing to be born. Personifying the place, he imagines it to be a woman. Its rank, orchidaceous fertility refutes any notion of a wise, sober, male creator, so he couples with it by making vegetable love, and thrusts his penis into a mossy crevice. Then, disgusted, he decides to stop wallowing, and for a while he establishes a stringent administrative regime, with time precisely allocated to chores and penalties imposed for infractions. At his most fanatical, he wishes he could enforce his edicts with corporal punishment or the death penalty – but that would mean flogging or executing himself, since he is the only citizen. When he reflects on the absurdity of this attempt at government, he recognizes that the island has exposed the fallacy of all social arrangements and legal or moral systems: they are an ineffectual attack on our own nature. Finally, thanks to a happy accident, the long toil of reconstructing civilization is aborted.

When Friday arrives on the island, Tournier's Crusoe at last has someone to rule. Power depends on capricious inequalities, so Friday is forbidden to use his master's stock of tobacco; but he smokes illicitly, sets fire to the ammunition in Crusoe's shelter, and incidentally blows up all his household goods. At this point, progress necessarily stalls, master and slave change places, and the island, no longer a workplace, becomes a playground. In this reckoning it is not Crusoe the writer but Friday who invents the idea of art, our adult continuation of childhood games. Friday unpacks a chest of clothes left from the wreck and arranges the courtly garments on some cacti, conjuring up a tatterdemalion company of lords and ladies; he guts a dead goat, ties and tunes the sinews, and makes an Aeolian harp. Now the aestheticized island truly qualifies as a holiday destination. Crusoe takes extended naps in his hammock, and is persuaded to expose his body to the sun or to sample exotic meals that Friday prepares by mixing meat and fish, sweet and sour. As if the island were a hotel, there is never any washing-up to do: the food cooks inside a skin of clay that hardens in the fire and can be smashed and thrown away when dinner is finished. A ship eventually arrives, and Friday – his 'Ariel spirit' entranced by the skimming, volatile thing – escapes on it. His replacement on the island is a kitchen boy who deserts his post and sneaks ashore. The elderly Crusoe calls his new companion and accomplice Sunday: a more

propitious name than Friday because, rather than marking the exhausted end
of the working week, it recalls a day given over to rest and recreation.

The piety of Defoe's Crusoe is deceptive. When he lectures Friday
about the origins of the world, he turns into God's surrogate, not his faithful
exegete. But what if Crusoe's story is read as a fable about the affinity between
Defoe and God, who like a novelist creates an island and sets on it a representative selection of human beings so that – as in Eden – he can examine
their moral worthiness? In Muriel Spark's novel *Robinson*, published in 1958,
a character looks askance at a rosary and comments: 'That's an R.C. item'.
Not coincidentally, the initials of Defoe's hero also stand for Roman Catholic.
Spark's Robinson is a renegade candidate for the priesthood who refused
ordination because he mistrusted the church's superstitions; settling in the
Azores, he follows his own heretical route towards 'spiritual advancement'.
He shares none of his namesake's economic concerns, and has not bothered
to cultivate his island or even to plant a kitchen garden; instead he relies on
a supply of tinned food. When a plane crashes on the island, he rescues and
shelters the few survivors. They owe him their lives, yet they turn against
him, maligning and apparently murdering him, after which they set up
a rough wooden cross to honour his memory. The creative experiment summarized in the Bible rushes ahead from the innocent garden to the crucifix raised
on a mound of skulls; Spark's story ends, it seems, with the sacrifice of God,
or at least that of his representative on earth. Shipwrecks are redundant, since
modern castaways fall from the air rather than being washed up on beaches.
The violent vertical arrival of Robinson's uninvited guests is announced by
a trail of fire, perhaps following the trajectory of the angels expelled from
heaven. The map printed in the novel makes the fable more explicit. The
island looks like a diagram of postlapsarian man, sprawled on the ocean
and still kicking in protest at his abasement: one outcrop is the Headlands,
beneath which North Arm and South Arm are flung out, with North Leg and

West Leg crookedly extending further along. 'No man is an island,' one of the characters derivatively remarks. The humanoid outline argues otherwise, and Spark's female narrator – a journalist with a commission to write a book about islands – has her own reasons for disagreeing with Donne's claim. 'Some are,' she says. 'Their only ground of meeting is concealed under the sea.' The peaks of the Azores are the summits of drowned mountains; they might also be the tips of Freudian icebergs, and if you follow them to their base you discover their interconnection – a sign of our complicity, like a stain spreading through the water.

The island has a hell prepared for malefactors: a sulphurous volcanic crater known as the Furnace, an excretory system for human and industrial waste. Robinson dumps his empty food tins here rather than tossing them into the ocean, whose regurgitations would toss them back onshore; as he balefully puts it, 'The Furnace is final'. For a while, it seems that he too might have been shoved into that pit. But he reappears, and explains why he absconded. The quarrelsome, vexatious people he saved from the plane had disrupted his peace, and after deciding that 'it would never do to keep a disorderly island' he simply wandered off and left humanity to its own devices. As on Good Friday, those he abandons immediately blame each other, and his resurrection does not expunge the evidence of this shared guilt. The novel wonders whether the creation – of that earthly island, and of the beings dropped onto it – might have been an error of judgment. If so, it is not irrevocable. Robinson's island is supposed to be an offshoot of Atlantis, still jutting out above the water; some time after her return to London, Spark's heroine reads in a newspaper that volcanic activity is causing it to sink. The story of Atlantis completes itself, although this time it has a Christian gloss: heaven, unattainable because we are undeserving, recedes under the water rather than drifting higher into the sky. The island is already, for Spark's character, 'a place of the mind', and she calls it 'apocryphal'. The word, chosen carefully, means hidden away – marginalized like the more questionable books of the Bible that are classified as the Apocrypha. An ocean has plenty of empty space in which to secrete such chunks of land.

The earth is forever making and unmaking islands, heaving them out of the water and sucking them back into it. Whereas Spark's novel ends with the reported death of an island (which sends Robinson off in search of 'some other isolation'), Bishop's poem about Crusoe begins with a complementary newspaper story in which 'some ship saw an island being born'. Steam apparently spouted from the ocean and a block of basalt was coughed up. The retired, repatriated Crusoe finds the idea exhausting. While on his island he had

> nightmares of other islands
> stretching away from mine, infinities
> of islands, islands spawning islands,
> like frogs' eggs turning into polliwogs
> of islands, knowing that I had to live
> on each and every one, eventually.

Polliwogs are tadpoles: the word pictures a spillage of seed wriggling on the water, as messily prolific as Polynesia. The old man – a character who through no fault or wish of his own became mythic, thanks to the variable ways in which novelists and poets retold his story – has the same polymorphous life, and would prefer to be relieved of it. His time on the island exponentiates into a series of life sentences, not served concurrently: to the first term of twenty-seven years are added the twenty-eight years of Tournier's Crusoe, the Swiss family's decade and the six-year vacation of Offenbach's Crusoé, plus the long weekend spent on a man-made island by Ballard's motorist. If only it were true, as Crusoe's female companion says in J. M. Coetzee's *Foe*, that 'all shipwrecks become the same shipwreck, all castaways the same castaways'.

But literature particularizes; the island becomes a local habitation, the mythic hero acquires a name. Does this mean that Crusoe himself is condemned to toil through the subsequent lives of his namesakes and imitators? Bishop's version of the man objects in principle: an island denotes singularity, and one ego ought to be enough.

2 KINGS OF CREATION

Edmond Dantès, the hero of Alexandre Dumas' *The Count of Monte Cristo*, is the most ruthlessly insular of men. His rancorous temperament is formed by his sufferings on one island; bent on revenge, he remakes himself in the image of another island. He is wrongly imprisoned on the Château d'If, a fortified outcrop on the smallest of the Frioul Islands, within sight of Marseilles. He escapes by pretending to be the corpse of another inmate; hurled into the sea, he surfaces near the island of Tiboulen, a projectile of lava that resembles 'a vast fire petrified at the moment of its most fervent combustion'. He clings to it during a storm, and fears that Tiboulen, thrashed by waves and seared by lightning, will come untethered and whisk him away. When he reaches the mainland he does not stay long, but buys the volcanic island of Monte Cristo between Corsica and Elba and nominates himself its Count. He models himself on this black eruption (though in his destruction of his enemies he expunges the mountain's forgiving Christian associations); he, like Tiboulen, is a synthesis of infuriated heat and implacable rigour. A snooty aristocrat points out that the so-called Count takes his title from a rock, which is hardly proof of noble lineage. But that is the point: islands denote uniqueness. 'He is an original, then?' asks a Paris gossip. Another commentator reports that the Count is 'somewhat eccentric'. His island is 'an atom in the infinite', a grain of sand afloat on the water. Even so, it confers lordship on him, makes him feel that he is 'king of all creation', and entitles him to play the role of an avenging angel. Romantic egotists like Dantès prefer ostracism to membership of the timid herd, and the islands they occupy are the settings for a new phase of our moral history.

In 1816 Byron sailed off into voluntary exile, spurning a society that hypocritically condemned his sexual adventures. At Dover, he looked over his shoulder without regret and noticed that, whereas other islands wavered in a blue haze, England's cliffs were white – spectral, funereal, as if his homeland were the isle of the dead or of those whose religion had left them only half-alive. The dissipated hero of *Childe Harold's Pilgrimage* follows Byron's example and haughtily quits 'the inviolate island of the sage and free'. There is a sarcastic slur in the phrase. Britain's natural defences may have made it unconquerable, but Byron, who did not feel free there, is at liberty to violate the place by mocking it. Writing to his mother during his first Mediterranean tour, he compared the burial mounds of Troy with 'the barrows of Danes in your Island'. It was hers not his; he looked for smaller, more exclusive places, where he would not be bothered by stuffy relatives or meddling gossips. On Cephalonia, his friend Trelawny reported that the Greeks favoured monarchical rule, and if they were to choose a foreign king would probably elect Byron. He reacted nonchalantly to the prospect, and joked that 'If it don't suit my humour, I shall, like Sancho, abdicate'. An island was all very well, so long as he could be relieved from the responsibility of governing it. A truly Byronic island had to be an autocracy – like Monte Cristo, a kingdom of one.

As he travelled, Byron revised geography to suit his psychological needs. Venice, where he lived for three years early in his exile, he described as 'the greenest island of my imagination'. The city is not an island, though it is perched on a subsiding archipelago, nor is it naturally green. What makes the metaphor work is Byron's intuitive link between imagination and the idea of an island, whose cultivated greenery is supplied by the poems it has inspired.

Looking at Venice, most of us fill in the gaps between the tufts and clumps of land – actually platforms balanced on tidal sandbars – that protrude from the lagoon. We interpret the canals as streets, thoroughfares connecting what we take to be islands. But Byron dissolved the shaky amalgam and chose to emphasize the unadhesive parts, not the wishful whole. When Childe Harold arrives in Venice, he begins by remarking that it rises out of the water as if impelled by an enchanter's wand, and concludes with a reminder that Venice sits 'in state, throned on her hundred isles!' Only Byron would have thought of numbering the islands and as soon as he does so the convention of urban unity founders. Can one throne extend to cover so many breakaway particles? The Doge, overseeing a maritime empire, aspired to be 'a ruler of the waters', but can an element be ruled? In Byron's play *Marino Faliero* this scepticism is voiced by a Doge as he plots to kill the senators who installed him in office: though he presides in his 'ducal state', he is only 'apparent sovereign of our hundred isles'. Sovereignty is an appearance, as is the deliquescent city. The conspirator Calendaro glances back at the origins of the state:

> Our fathers did not fly from Attila
> Into these isles, where palaces have sprung
> On banks redeem'd from the rude ocean's ooze,
> To own a thousand despots in his place.

The rudeness of the ooze argues against the possibility of redemption; the palaces wobble, and the hundred islands – each potentially the domain of a disgruntled individual – spawn a thousand egomaniacal dictators. What fascinated Byron about Venice was its infirmity, which he identified with the swampy laxity of our buried lives. Yet he set himself to uphold the façade, to clamp together the disparate islands that moulder under water. This is how Harold situates himself in the city:

> I stood in Venice, on the Bridge of Sighs;
> A palace and a prison on each hand.

He is the bridge between gaudy luxury and the submarine agony of the dungeon; the palatial and the penitential, though relegated to separate islands, are two of his indwelling selves. Israel Bertuccio in *Marino Faliero* does not stand on the bridge, statically balancing power and misery, but crosses it and travels from one extreme to the other. As he moves between upper and lower worlds, he rejoices that his is the last sigh that will ever

> echo o'er the Stygian wave which flows
> Between the murderers and the murder'd, washing
> The prison and the palace walls.

A metaphor has again transformed the topography. The canal is now a river, a tributary of the Styx, and the waves that slap against the walls are agents of erasure and oblivion, the means by which death cleanses the world.

A man on an island detaches himself from others, perhaps even from the fluent continuum of life itself. This is why Wordsworth insisted that 'We must live/ Not in Utopia.../ Or some secreted island heaven knows where', but in an ordinary, convivial world, shared with others. Islands fatally disrupt that social covenant. Nietzsche in *The Gay Science* remarked that the mountains near Portofino, abruptly shelving towards the Mediterranean, 'plunge into the sea with a proud and measured tranquillity' while 'the Gulf of Genoa sings its melody to the end'. Seen like this, an island is a suicidal mountain, and the islands favoured by Byron doubled as possible necropoli. Leaving for his second journey to Greece, he had a 'presentiment' that he would die there, and he did his best, long before the illness that killed him at Missolonghi in 1824, to ensure that this happened. He decreed his death and rehearsed it, experimenting with apt locations. Visiting a monastery on Cephalonia, he lowered himself into a sarcophagus and began declaiming Hamlet's address to the skull. On another occasion he told Trelawny that he wished to be buried on 'a rocky islet off Maina – it is the Pirates' Isle; it suggested *The Corsair*. No one knows it'. In his poem about the marauding buccaneer Conrad, he calls it a 'lonely isle'. Aloneness is the arrogant prerogative of such places.

The rocky islet suggested *The Corsair* because, like Monte Cristo, its stark jagged profile characterizes the hero whose headquarters it is. Retreating from fellowship, Conrad possesses a stony insentience. When he is captured and tortured, Byron testifies that 'He deeply, darkly felt', although he refuses to admit his vulnerability and sleeps in his chains. As he sails home with his crew at twilight, 'the very rocks appear to smile' – but the geological welcome is a mere appearance projected onto the adamantine barrier. Hoarse, shrieking birds encircle the island, and on arriving Conrad finds the body of his dead lover Medora. His tearful collapse almost embarrasses Byron, who comments that 'His heart was form'd for softness': hearts are feeble, squashy organs, too easily hurt, which is why rock represents a stoical immunity to pain. Conrad's career has left him

> sunk, and chill'd, and petrified at last.
> Yet tempests wear, and lightning cleaves the rock;
> If such his heart, so shatter'd it the shock.

He disappears, and his followers conduct a search of 'mount, grotto, cavern, valley', as if he had literally petrified. That would be an appropriate end, because a pun at the beginning of the poem treats the corsair as a corpse, a stiff husk containing defunct emotion like an urn with its store of ashes:

> His corse may boast its urn and narrow cave,
> And they who loath'd his life may gild his grave.

Actually he has put out to sea again, choosing to wander remorsefully on a lachrymose lake of grief. As the carousing pirates put it,

> Ours are the tears, though few, sincerely shed,
> When Ocean shrouds and sepulchres our dead.

Byron's morbid geography offers a choice between two graves: skeletal adhesion to the island's rock, or dissolution in the water around it.

A song in the third canto of *Don Juan* celebrates 'the isles of Greece' as the 'place of birth' for gods, muses, heroes and lovers. Yet those islands are also sites of extinction. Byron inevitably remembers Sappho's leap from her cliff on Lesbos, and perhaps imagines imitating her when he recalls his visit to Sounion, a tip of the Attic peninsula that is not quite an island since it still clings to the mainland:

> Place me on Sunium's marbled steep,
>   Where nothing, save the waves and I,
> May hear our mutual murmurs sweep;
>   There, swan-like, let me sing and die.

The death-wish expressed itself in a memento he left behind at Sounion in 1810, when he carved his name at the base of Poseidon's temple. The man who defaces a monument in this way crassly marks his presence but also commemorates his eventual absence; whereas Poseidon rules over the forgetful element of water, Byron has eternally embedded himself in the rock. After a shipwreck, Don Juan is washed up on 'one of the wild and smaller Cyclades', which gives Byron an excuse to disparage the myth that made the Cyclades a cosmic centre. 'Some of these,' he points out, 'are rocks with scarce a hut on', and he jokes about the 'oxless isles', unable to feed cattle although sheep and goats can graze on their scant vegetation. But Juan's profaned island has another psychological use: as well as saving his life, it confirms the possibility that we can exist as individuals, belonging to neither the continent nor the main. For someone at the mercy of undifferentiated water,

> Lovely seem'd any object that should sweep
> Away the vast, salt, dread, eternal deep.

The island refutes the oceanic flux, that gulf of non-being. Life may have begun in the water, as Byron implies by saying that the quiescent Mediterranean 'slumber'd like an unwean'd child', but man – an island of loamy flesh and flinty bone – needs attachment to the earth. Or has Juan simply advanced from one death to another? He is resurrected in this 'place of pleasure', but his infatuated rescuer Haidée, gazing at him with eyes 'black as death', sees him as a nubile cadaver, sleeping 'like a top, or like the dead'. When he revives, she is amazed by 'such appetite in one she had deem'd dead': could his ardour be vampiric? She is just as disconcerted by the return of her father Lambro, lost at sea and also given up for dead. Lambro is outraged to discover his 'hearthstone turn'd into a tomb', and finds the revelation of his daughter's affair with Juan harder than 'the mental pangs of dying'. She asserts that 'I love him – I will die with him'; it amounts to the same thing. After a convulsion in which a vein bursts, she hardens into a classical statue, an 'exquisitely chisell'd' effigy whose body immures a child that goes 'down to the grave unborn'. On Byron's metaphysical islands, life and death change places, with art equivocally positioned between them.

In 1823 Byron wrote a narrative poem about the *Bounty* mutineers, entitled – in a succinct admission of what interested him – *The Island; or, Christian and his Comrades*. First comes the island, a 'sea-green' Polynesian Eden; the islanders, who gain access to this 'guilt-won paradise' by committing a crime, are secondary. The island in question is Pitcairn, which has turned out to be less idyllic than the 'yet infant world' of erotic delight imagined by Byron: the inbred descendants of the *Bounty* mutineers are still holed up there, sexually abusing underage girls and claiming (as did the seven men who were put on trial in 2004) that local custom sets the age of consent at twelve. Byron thought of islands as citadels for a lonely hero, accompanied perhaps by a woman who, like Medora or Haidée, conveniently dies after consummation. It did not occur to him that an island as small as Pitcairn had the same disadvantages as the Britain he had spurned: it was a closed society, as inescapable as a family, and those within its borders, unable to go elsewhere for fear of arrest, could only quarrel like the feuding *Bounty* mutineers. Two antithetical Byronic heroes fight it out on his version of Pitcairn. Christian is another of Byron's brooding moral outlaws, like Harold the irreligious pilgrim or Conrad the corsair. But the young sailor Torquil, a Hebridean islander sexually awakened on this warmer island where he mates with the native girl Neuha, is closer to Don Juan; he is a child of nature innocently suckled by a land where bread grows on trees like fruit and perpetual summer arouses the unclad flesh. One story is inevitably tragic, since it is about the implosion of an embittered mind. The other is a comedy that outsmiles death and looks forward to the perpetuation of happiness. Does Pitcairn have room for both?

Because Byron's Christian spends his time aloof, statuesquely inflexible in his resolve, there is little the poem can do except liken him to the island, which when he occupies the foreground is stark and stony, not the lush jungle through which Torquil romps with Neuha. He is 'obdurate as a portion of the rock', and his mood is that of 'an extinct volcano': his mind is the conical crater, with the ancient fires of resentment buried far below the waterline. Like a peak, he is 'of a higher order' as he looms above his swinish comrades. His morose solitude prompts Byron to reinflect the familiar yet enigmatic notion of the desert island. Does the designation mean that such places are wastes of sand, or does it perhaps conceal an accusation? Captain Bligh brooded about this during his long voyage to Timor after the mutineers set him adrift; he decided that the rebels, being 'void of connexions', were the kind of men who 'would have been tempted to desert. ... Desertions have happened...from most of the ships that have been at the Society Islands'. In Bligh's judicial vocabulary, a desert island was the lair of deserters. Byron has a different idea, and refers to a spar of rock that pokes through the surf near 'the isle of Toobonai' as 'a desert to mankind'. The absence of human beings is the advantage of such a place.

When the naval scouts discover Christian's hideout and hunt him down, he is the last of the mutineers to die: death, in Byron's estimation, is an aristocratic privilege not a lowly common fate, and the hero is reluctant to share it with lesser men. Twice wounded, Christian dies fighting, and when he runs out of ammunition he tears a button from his vest, stuffs it in the muzzle of his gun, then fires it and kills an adversary. After this, shaking his fist in rage, he leaps from a cliff. Byron aggrandized the more sordid truth. Christian was actually murdered during a dispute between the mutineers and the Tahitians whose women they had commandeered; it was one of his surviving comrades who unheroically tumbled over a cliff, stupefied by liquor from a homemade still. As Byron reconceives it, Christian's death incorporates him into the island:

the rock below received like glass
His body crush'd into one gory mass,
With scarce a shred to tell of human form,
Or fragment for the sea-bird or the worm.

It is the ultimate act of self-glorifying self-elimination. He kills himself to prevent others doing so, and cleverly pulverizes his corpse to frustrate posthumous judgment.

Torquil dies too, but his expiry is the brief aftermath of sexual bliss, from which he soon recovers. He and Neuha flee from the invaders and go to ground in their own inaccessible, water-walled island. They plunge into the ocean and appear to drown, but after their dive they soar upwards through the waves into a cavern vaulted like a cathedral, with stalactites cheekily mimicking mitres and crucifixes. No prim, disapproving god dwells beneath this 'self-born Gothic canopy'; Byron identifies the creative agent as Darkness, a goddess who has scooped the enwombing cavity from inside her body. The sanctuary is 'a central realm of earth', despite its lack of 'tree, and field, and sky', and here Neuha – who in converting Torquil to noble savagery has 'civilized Civilization's son!' – performs once again the feat of Promethean magic that makes culture possible. A little improbably, she unwraps a pine torch, a plantain leaf, a flint and some twigs, all of which she has kept dry in her bosom, and uses this equipment to kindle fire. Although Christian's volcano has expired, here in Neuha's 'subterranean world' a new life is incubated.

Beneath the surface Byron finds mementos of a time when the earth was molten and a creative chaos gave birth to islands. The cavern's architrave was formed by an earthquake, and the buttress separated from a mountain

When the Poles crash'd, and water was the world;
Or harden'd from some earth-absorbing fire,

While yet the globe reek'd from its funeral pyre.

In the Pacific, intermittently speckled by islands like Pitcairn, the world still consists of water, and as the investigating fleet sails away Neuha rejoices to see the evidence of alien humanity expunged: 'All was ocean, all was joy!' If all is ocean, the island has retreated into the depths, reversing its own violent nativity. Or perhaps it has rebounded into the air, like anchorless Delos. Above 'the studded archipelago' Byron sees 'the starry isles', which might be the pinpricks of innumerable alternative earths that spill across the dark, deep sky of the southern hemisphere – an aerial Polynesia, offering the homeless refugee a choice of worlds.

Romantic fantasy scoured the globe for sulking retreats like Pitcairn. Hence Scott's attraction to the Orkneys, which he saw as castaway splinters of Scandinavia. In *The Pirate*, Hoy, 'that mountain of an island', consists of three pinnacles with clefts or chasms between them; its soil is 'sterile', allowing a toehold only to a few dwarfish bushes. What home could be more suitable for a social outcast? Scott considered piracy to be a romantic trade, a result of secession like the breach that detaches islands from continents. In Cowper's translation of *The Odyssey*, Cyclops asks the dilatory hero

> from what distant shore
> Roam ye the waters? traffic ye? or bound
> To no one port, wander, as pirates use,
> At large the Deep...?

But the true romantic buccaneer does more than wander. He is a revolutionary, who operates outside the law to redress wrongs and to combat the profiteering of oppressive empires. Scott's heroine Minna fondly imagines her remote Viking ancestors assailing the frontiers of 'degenerate Rome' in their long galleys.

Cleveland, a Byronic corsair who hides in the Orkneys, blames or perhaps thanks another island, a scrubby key in the West Indies, for forming his character. He grew up on 'the little island of Tortuga' in the Caribbean; the Spaniards plundered his family's plantation, and his father recruited a band of rovers to seize back the stolen treasure. Cleveland fell out with this mutinous crew, and was marooned on Coffin-key in the Bermudas, 'a speck of unproductive sand, surrounded by the boundless Atlantic', inhabited only by turtles, boobies and the demons worshipped in voodoo cults. He spent four weeks there, and during that time he demystified or exorcized the place. Often in the morning mist he was accosted by spectres, but when the air cleared he always discovered the phantoms to be bushes or clumps of drift-wood. Solitude toughened him, teaching him to renounce humane feelings: 'on that spot of barren sand I found, or rather forged, the iron mask which has since been my chief security'.

The image of the forge announces Cleveland's advance beyond Crusoe, who can only work with wood or mould clay; he has almost anticipated the achievement of Verne's engineers, who arrive at 'the metallic period' when they extract coal and ore from a mountain on their island. But Cleveland's forge is mental, like the furnace of the brain in Blake's poem about the tiger, and when the fire of contempt for mankind cools, it leaves him with a metallized face, debarring emotion. Scott has predicted the next mutation of the stoical Byronic hero, who made his first official appearance twenty years later when Dumas published *The Man in the Iron Mask*.

The iron mask clamped over the head of Dumas' anonymous nobleman is a literal visor. It has springs of steel at the chin, which enable the prisoner to eat; he has to shave without removing it, so he extracts hairs from his beard with tweezers. According to David Coward, this cruel, impractical punishment was the consequence of a pun, or of verbal slips that accumulated as the legend was retold during the eighteenth century. A mask of cloth became a mask of 'vair' (fur), which was mistranscribed as 'verre' (glass) and eventually warped into 'fer' (iron); the succession of errors propped up the myth. The actual prisoner – a victim of intrigues at the court of Louis XIV, possibly the monarch's illegitimate son – served his term in the Bastille, but it seemed logical to transfer him from the city to an island fortress. Here he could suffer inside a trebly reinforced prison, with water, stone and metal conspiring to isolate him. When Mark Twain visited the Château d'If he saw the dungeon supposedly occupied by the man in the iron mask, whose 'speechless tongue' left his mind a 'closed book'. It was of course Dantès in *The Count of Monte Cristo* who had been incarcerated there; Mark Twain's wishful thinking made the two characters cellmates.

The island that serves as a synonym for Dantès is, however, Monte Cristo not the Château d'If. The cone of rock projecting from the sea is the spout of a dormant volcano; fire glimmers from it, possibly lit by pirates encamped there. A visitor to Monte Cristo, transfixed by this glare, calls the island a 'terrestrial star', and fancies that it might be a meteor fatally lunging to earth: another image, like the volcano, of the burned-out romantic temperament. The Count dopes his guest with hashish and conducts him into what he calls Aladdin's Cave, furnished with divans over which are draped the skins of lions, tigers, panthers, bears and foxes – wildness gutted and transformed into pampered comfort. From outside, the Count may appear, like the bristling rock, to be a figure of nocturnal menace and incipient violence. Within, sealed in the island's scented, opiate interior, he is a voluptuary. From a distance, Monte Cristo is the blasted aftermath of an eruption, or the remnant of some astral calamity. Once you probe deeper, the desert island turns into an oasis: its vaulted store of riches makes it, as the Count says, an Oriental paradise, where he lolls like a satiated pasha. The two aspects of the place bring together the opposed identities of the Byronic hero, both a self-destructive wreck and a self-indulgent libertine.

Excavated to make room for the Count's plush apartments and his hoard of treasure, the island is a hollow, fragile bubble of fantasy. The same is true of another fantastical island in *The Man in the Iron Mask*. Fouquet, the corrupt adviser of Louis XIV, has raided the state's coffers to fortify Belle-Île-en-Mer off Brittany, installing defensive ditches and aiming two hundred cannons at potential invaders. He pretends to be strengthening a bastion against the English or the Dutch; actually he is preparing a power base from which he can challenge the king. When the three musketeers are accused of conspiring with Fouquet, Athos admits that he betrayed their communal code: 'My crime was being an egotist'. Where better than an island to commit it? The musketeers reconvene in a grotto at Locmaria to undermine Fouquet's scheme, and set off explosives in a cavern that was once, Dumas claims, a temple to carnivorous Celtic gods who required human sacrifices; this time the earth itself gobbles up Porthos. His end is 'the death of a Titan', but although he tosses mountains around like the classical Titans, he cannot prevent one of them from becoming his sepulchre. The detonation reproduces the primal catastrophe that forms Neuha's cave in Byron's poem: the sky tumbles down in 'a chaos more confused, more shapeless, more terrible than the chaos which existed an hour before God had created the world', and after its collapse there remains 'nothing by which God could have known His own work'. God, in fact, has been deposed. Romantic man is his own god; like Dantès, Fouquet or Verne's engineers, he stakes his claim to creative primacy by adapting and embellishing an island. The Count of Monte Cristo wants, he says, to make 'a life of dreams and a paradise of realities'. Perhaps such perfection is denied to us, either by an insulted deity or by the laws and limits of nature. Atlantis founders, and in the gulf at Locmaria the world is uncreated.

Napoleon Bonaparte, the Corsican upstart who imperiously redesigned the map of the world, was born on one island and died on another. In between, he ruled a continent. After his abdication in 1814, he was granted Elba in the Mediterranean as his residence; Byron sarcastically commemorated the romantic hero's fall by telling him to hasten to the 'sullen Isle,/ And gaze upon the sea', which he had never conquered. The victors awarded him sovereignty on Elba, and he said he intended to settle down into being a justice of the peace. Despite this vow, within a year he returned to the mainland and shakily re-established his power for a hundred days. Abdicating a second time, he wanted to sail to America, but the British insisted on banishing him to their colony of St Helena in the South Atlantic. The monotony of his routine on the bare island was calculated to corrode an aspiring mind; he died there in 1821. Reconsidering the emperor's fate in the 1860s, Victor Hugo remarked that 'total ruin is like Waterloo' whereas 'slow decline is St Helena', and argued that 'the diminution of Napoleon diminished Britain'.

By then Hugo was himself an exiled islander. When Prince Louis Napoleon dispensed with the Assembly in 1851, he left Paris for Brussels, then crossed to the Channel Islands. He lived on Jersey until 1855; expelled for insulting Queen Victoria, he moved to Guernsey, which he called his 'rock of hospitality'. There he remained until the restoration of the Republic in 1870. He felt at home because the islands themselves were exiles, crumbs of Normandy that had been washed out to sea, and he hoped – as he bombarded the mainland with denunciations of the new Emperor and incendiary tracts wrapped in the leaves of cigars or stuffed inside dead chickens – that they would be in the vanguard of his campaign to liberate France. His friend Auguste Vacquerie, less optimistic, likened St Helier to St Helena, and as he plodded round in trapped circles declared: 'I hate islands'.

While Hugo waited for the empire to fall, he contemplated the ocean like Byron's Napoleon, and – along with epic poems, plays and a study of Shakespeare – wrote *The Toilers of the Sea*, published in 1866. He dedicated the novel to 'the noble little people of Guernsey', whose industrious skill in resisting the ocean had constructed 'a laborious human anthill', a busy midden made in the image of grimacing Caliban, with rocks that erupted into tumours, cysts and warts. *The Toilers of the Sea* begins with an anthropological survey of the archipelago, during which Hugo casually remarks that he owns one of the more negligible islets in the group, an alluvial deposit of sand held in place by a patch of grass, sold to him for three francs by the farmer who claimed to own the freehold. Guernsey at least has a sustainable economy: Hugo's definition of a habitable island is a place that has food sources and fresh water, with land for pasturing sheep, goats or cattle. This model community probably also has a functioning press. Noting that Jersey and Guernsey had ten newspapers between them, Hugo joked that the day after Crusoe arrived on his desert island he would set about publishing a journal, with Friday as his single loyal subscriber. Sceptical of the 'irreducible English instinct' to establish a safe, closed circle of writing and reading, Hugo set the central episode of his novel on a reef, an exiguous barrier of naked rock that is, as he specifies, 'not an island'. Here the fisherman Gilliatt, stranded after a shipwreck, performs a task harder than Crusoe's long, patient labour of construction, cultivation and manufacture. He single-handedly disassembles the wrecked ship and extracts the engine. He sets up a forge in a cave, and harnesses the elements to make it work: the wreck provides fuel, the keening wind supplies bellows, and the source of power is his own inexhaustible will. He makes the tools he needs from spars of timber and scraps of metal. After two months of solitary labour, he lowers the engine from the reef where it is pinioned and sails it back to Guernsey on a raft he has fabricated for the purpose. In his spare time, he battles a storm and fends off a leviathan. He hopes that these efforts will earn him the love of the ship-owner's daughter; by the time he returns, however, she has chosen another.

The surgery Gilliatt performs on the ship is an act of industrial engineering. Its ingenuity makes it a work of art (Hugo calls the contrivance Gilliatt's 'masterpiece'), and like all art, it is a feat of metaphysical bravado. The pillars in the sea, two uprights with an architrave gripped between them, form a 'huge capital *H*'; one rock in the group is known as Homme, anthropomorphized because the body of a shipwrecked man was once found on top of it, surrounded by shells from which he had gouged scraps of food. Gilliatt strings a knotted cord between the standing stones and uses it to swing across from one to the other. This is not quite man tightrope-walking above the abyss – the metaphysical spectacle imagined by Nietzsche – but it is almost equally impressive, because Gilliatt gains a foothold on a granitic summit where 'no creature without wings' has ever trodden. Hugo describes the flat-topped rocks as 'peaks that have been decapitated'. Like headless men, they embody the brutish stupor of the world before it is humanized; Gilliatt, thinking his way through obstructions, asserts the primacy of mind. Robert Louis Stevenson, an expert on islands, believed that Hugo had given a truer account of man's place in the universe than Defoe was able to do. After reading *The Toilers of the Sea* he dismissed *Robinson Crusoe* as a product of 'the old days before art had learnt to occupy itself with what lies outside of human will'; it is a blinkered book, limited by a humanism that made Defoe's hero the 'sole centre of interest in the midst of a nature utterly dead and utterly unrealized by the artist'. On his reef Gilliatt does more than mould pots and reinvent the umbrella. He has to contend with nature's active hostility or malevolence, as sea-birds circle to mock his efforts while they wait to feed on his corpse.

Sharing Gilliatt's defiance, Hugo did not surrender to that animosity. He viewed the universe as 'a mass of raw material', but within that draughty, incoherent immensity he situated 'the world, which is God's work and man's canvas'. The world we mark out as a habitat is our shared island, like neat, quarried Guernsey. Gilliatt wins a principled victory over elemental chaos, and his achievement is not diminished when, after renouncing any claim on the ship-owner's daughter, he uncomplainingly commits suicide. For two impassive hours he sits on a pinnacle offshore that is engulfed by the incoming tide, and as the chilly water makes its way up his body, he calmly watches the lovers who will survive him as they exchange endearments back on dry land. Consciousness detaches itself from the foundering, drowning organism; his head, before it goes under, is a lighthouse of resolute clarity and sacrificial altruism. A moment later, as Hugo declares in the last sentence of the novel, 'There was now nothing but the sea.' In *The Island*, Byron similarly remembers a time when 'water was the world'. The poem jauntily reconciles itself to the erasure of human life, since people are only flotsam; the novel more movingly laments nature's stealthy obliteration of this irreplaceable man – an island of light and warmth, of intelligence and affection, now uncreated and reabsorbed into the formless flux.

10: ISLANDERS AND EGGS

Crusoe's island was a school of self-reliance, where only a man who was physically strong and mentally tough could survive. But when Rousseau recommended the novel to young Emile, he foresaw the new use to which it would soon be put: boys took over the island. Romanticism dispelled the terrors of the place by pacifying nature; its poetry prolonged childhood, drawing on reserves of delight that dry up in most of us when we become adults. In effect this meant continuing to live on the island, since the passage home promised only the dreary assumption of grown-up responsibilities. Jim Hawkins explores a world that is renovated by his childish capacity for wonder, so that he seems – in a phrase that recalls the Edenic freshness of creation – to be the first visitor 'since the island rose out of the sea'. His ingenuous poetic imagination protects him from its perils, as if in a cocoon of words. A snake, irritated by his intrusion, hisses 'with a noise not unlike the spinning of a top'. The charmingly childish metaphor saves Jim from noticing that it is a rattler, so he doesn't realize until later, perhaps with doomed, elderly hindsight, that he has brushed against 'a deadly enemy'. Marianne Moore defined poems as imaginary gardens containing real toads. Islands like this, however, are imaginary gardens in which even the snakes are imaginary. Or else the snakes living on such islands have wriggled free of the biblical curse. The Galápagos iguanas prompted Darwin to joke about the fable that blamed a snake for our original sin. The fifteen islets that made up the archipelago were, he declared, a 'paradise for the whole family of reptiles'.

The defining account of this idyllic island – our charmed home until adolescence induces a fall – is R. M. Ballantyne's *The Coral Island*, published in 1857. For a century it was compulsory for young readers, and it was one of the first books I owned. Its popularity meant that eventually it had to be undercut and satirically corrected: in *Lord of the Flies* Golding borrowed from Ballantyne the names of his two main characters, Ralph and Jack, who on their own tropical island preside over the swift degeneration of some stranded schoolboys into bloodthirsty savages. Golding's novel was set for study in my last year at school, officially ending the age of innocence. Forewarned, I put away my copy of Ballantyne, and only unearthed it on a return visit to Tasmania thirty years later.

The Coral Island is *Robinson Crusoe* blithely rewritten for juveniles. The menace of solitude and silence is waived: Ballantyne deposits three castaways on the coral reef, so they team up to help and comfort each other. Ralph Rover and his friends Jack and Peterkin are free to amuse themselves, since – nourished by breadfruit trees, with coconuts dispensing milk – they can survive without working. 'I am not of a mechanical turn', shrugs Ralph, unashamed that he lacks Crusoe's talents as an engineer. The boys occupy themselves in play, a naïve and instinctive form of art. They take their cue from the 'gambols' of the leaping porpoises in their lagoon, at once an athletic exercise and a graceful dance. As well as expending energy and passing the pointless time, their games conduct mental experiments that redesign the universe. Ralph collects fish and keeps them in a tank where salt and fresh water are mixed; Jack calls this little aquarium 'a miniature Pacific'. Given the ocean's dismaying immensity, to reduce its volume is a brave and cunning achievement. The tank is artfully embellished with fronds of seaweed, sand and gravel, which make it a stage-set for its performing occupants. As this decor reveals, the boys graduate more quickly than Crusoe from use to beauty, or from arduous function to otiose form. When they befriend a native, they give him a rusty axe, the tool that announces the advance of civilization. Their other offerings have a more sophisticated significance: they hand over 'a piece of wood with our names carved on it, and a piece of string to hang it round his neck as an ornament'. That string defines the wood as something precious; art's purpose is to publicize or immortalize the artist, and they manage this without needing to carve the block into any other shape.

The ocean and the island have a soporific influence, suspending the stress that is the consequence of our lives in time. Ralph is a believer in the therapeutic value of 'profound rest', so the boys devote extended intervals to dozing. The Pacific for once justifies its name, and lulls them like an amniotic ocean. Circumnavigating their island in a boat, they float 'placidly on the long oily swell', and take pleasure in 'the motion of the deep'. In the becalmed humidity of summer, nature apparently nods off, and the only proof of life is a 'long, deep breathing' audible in the rhythm of the sea. There is a lyrical sorcery in these descriptions: soothed by repetition, time goes to sleep. But despite Ballantyne's efforts to frustrate change, there are biological signs of an inevitable end. He does his best to preserve innocence by policing his diction. Why else does Ralph remark that the island is 'belted by a beach of pure white sand, on which laved the gentle ripples of the lagoon'? It would surely be better to say that the island was 'girdled', which is the word Coleridge used to describe Kubla Khan's walled pleasure garden; but this, combined with the lapping or licking of the waves, would have been intolerably sensuous. The girdle that accentuates female contours is replaced by the belt, a piece of male kit that keeps our trousers up. Such denials stylistically mimic the interdictions of local custom, signalled – as Ralph learns – by the word 'tabu'. The concept of taboo was one of Polynesia's bequests to modern consciousness: for Freud it signified emotional ambivalence, a blend of fascination and dread that is encoded, as he puts it in *Totem and Taboo*, in unwritten laws. Ballantyne's writing already flirts with those edicts, and the language that he tries to regiment sometimes blabs unruly secrets. Sex, suppressed in one place, makes itself felt elsewhere. Thus the rising sun sends light on a foray across 'the bosom of the broad Pacific', and a sailor raunchily sexes the anchor as he tosses it overboard: 'There, lass, take a good nap now, for we shan't ask you to kiss the mud again for many a long day to come!' She will kiss the mud only when saying goodbye, after being reluctantly tugged out of her mucky bed. The growing boys venture into tricky terrain when Peterkin, who disdains the use of a club, cuts a swathe of wood and sharpens it into a spear. 'If length constitutes power,' comments Jack, 'you'll certainly be invincible.' Before long, an element of priapic rivalry will surely creep into their games.

An island, where space limits our freedom of selection, interferes with the customary assumption that a man needs a woman. The saboteur who arranges the shipwreck in *The Toilers of the Sea* is stranded on a rock that hardly qualifies as an island. Hugo ponders the dualistic temperament of the hypocrite and wryly congratulates him for overcoming the biological challenge of the place: Clubin 'is a demon of double sex, the abominable hermaphrodite of evil. He fertilizes himself; he engenders himself.' A man has reverted to the miserable singleness of a protozoon, conducting his affairs by fission not fusion. Ballantyne's boys are not so perversely involuted, but they cannot help noticing how nature shrewdly contrives to continue life without recourse to sexual reproduction. They are intrigued by the banyan tree, which manages to be both singular and multiple, extruding fibres that

take root and develop as independent growths. In Ralph's aquarium a crab
sheds its shell and totters away from the body it has discarded, as if there
were two of it not one. Such tricks, however, cannot prevent the world's
imminent division into male and female principles. The blood-brothers
team up one last time to rescue a Samoan girl from the cannibals; although
it is a purely chivalrous act, it puts an end to play by acknowledging that
in the future they will be forced apart by more urgent, complex desires
and loyalties. During their circumnavigation, Peterkin suggests that 'we
continue our journey as fast as possible, lest our island should be converted
into a dream before we get completely round it'. What alarms him is the
possibility of rationalization: they have just found that what they mistook
for screeching spectres are only penguins, and too many such realizations or
decipherments will eject them from the fantasy. The comment expresses the
temporal panic that motivates romantic poetry. Can the vision be translated
into words before it fades? Will writing destroy an emotion by making
it articulate?

The boys return to what Peterkin calls 'the ancient Paradise'; they also
regress to a kind of shared womb. Wordsworth believed in a prenatal paradise
from which we fall when we are born, and he likened our indistinct memory
of it to an inland ocean: perhaps the coral island floats on that subliminal sea.
According to Wordsworth, we revisit our embryonic Eden in dreams, and
Ralph, who swoons when he is tossed ashore from the wrecked ship, awakens
on an island that seems like his blurred reverie. He enjoys 'a sort of dreamy,
confused consciousness; a half-waking, half-sleeping condition'. Has he died
and been transported to the island of the blessed? But this is not the post-
mortem journey undertaken by the figures in Böcklin's painting or Woolf's
novel; it is a rebirth, though of an unspiritual kind. Ralph is aware that missionaries are colonizing the Pacific and bringing 'the gospel of our Saviour'
to some 'favoured isles', but the coral island has escaped such ministrations.

His mother gives him a Bible to take to sea. Unlike Crusoe, he leaves it on the sinking ship, perhaps aware of its irrelevance.

Rebirth for the boys involves being unborn, squirming back into an aquarium inside the body. Their hiding place is a cave that is reached through an underwater tunnel, as narrow and dangerous as the birth canal. Peterkin is terrified of this backwards rite of passage, and has to be tugged through the aperture by his companions. Is this Wordsworth's benign drama or the re-enactment of a primal trauma, the reversal of our first protesting arrival in the world? When Ralph goes missing, Peterkin has to get out of the cave with only Jack to help him. This is the labour of our first emergence into the world, and Peterkin is prepared for it by being turned into a corpse: Jack ties his hands and feet, then lashes him to a long pole to keep him stiff, so he can be dragged through the channel. 'White as a dead man', he is 'as stiff and straight as an Egyptian mummy'. Is Jack the psychopomp, conducting him to a nether realm? No, their destination is the bright day-lit world above ground. Although Jack calls their safe transit a 'happy deliverance', midwives might say it was a delivery, complicated by the kicks Peterkin aims at the tunnel's roof as he is dragged along. And their revival is the resumption of grief and mourning: convinced that Ralph is dead, they set off to look for his body. While rescuing the Samoan girl, the boys stumble into a tribal temple littered with human bones and skulls and see a sacrificial victim being buried alive. The novel offers a stark choice between the womb and the mortuary.

As Ralph travels back to the island across 'the wide Pacific' on a schooner, he half-quotes Milton's *Paradise Lost*. 'The world lies before us,' he tells a fellow sailor, just as, when Adam and Eve quit the garden, 'the world was all before them'. Ralph's phrase has a jaunty, buoyant inflection; Milton's depressed preview of the calamitous history that lies ahead is an echoing premonition that Ralph himself may not be able to hear. Eventually the boys recognize that they have outlived the island, and head home to England. 'To part,' Ralph

announces, 'is the lot of all mankind'. Their wistful departure subtly muddles
time and space: they are saying farewell to a period of life, though they
separate themselves from it by treating it as a place and sailing away towards
manhood. We have no choice but to grow in time and finally to die. But we can
make choices about the space we occupy, so Ralph and his friends volunteer
to renounce paradise before they are expelled.

Ballantyne's boys leave the island before sexual knowledge arrives to perturb
them and to make them reconsider their choice of playmates. Puberty was
forestalled until 1908, when Henry De Vere Stacpoole – a ship's doctor who
knew the South Seas well – published his titillating fantasy *The Blue Lagoon*,
which leaves two shipwrecked cousins, a boy and a girl, to ripen into adolescence without being rescued. Their island southeast of the Marquesas is closed
off from external influences and from conventional disapproval. When a
cyclone lashes it, the wind sounds like 'a great multitude of people': Emmeline
and Dick have more to fear from society and its moralizing consensus than
from the enraged elements. Knowing no sin, they make love; a child is born
without pain or guilt. Their offspring is a boy, though they call him Hannah.
Are they paying inadvertent tribute to the androgyny of nature itself?

The film of *The Blue Lagoon* made in 1980 could afford to be explicit
about their carnal self-discovery. Brooke Shields is mystified by her menstrual
flow, and Christopher Atkins cannot understand why strange hairs are sprout-
ing on him. He experiences a flush of Crusoe-like achievement when he works
out how to masturbate: hands can be used for something more pleasurable
than carving wood or shaping clay! Stacpoole is more evasive, and overlooks
the nakedness of his characters. 'The climate,' he tactfully remarks, 'was a
suit of clothes in itself.' Once at least he does venture into territory that was
still officially unmentionable: when the children are set adrift in an open boat
with the old sailor who is their minder, the narrator comments that 'the most

terrible experience when cast away…is the total absence of privacy', which licenses us to speculate about how bodily functions are discharged when there are no doors to close. Otherwise Stacpoole, like Ballantyne, incorporates the prohibitions of local religion into his text, leaving a gap when Emmeline spontaneously delivers her baby or when two warring tribes spend a night massacring each other. These omissions correspond to the 'line…drawn across the beach' by the natives, 'beyond which there were no footmarks: that meant that the rest of the island was for some reason tabu'. In the film, Atkins romps in a skimpy loincloth, and Shields, dandling her infant, finds by fumbling trial and error that her breasts are not merely decorative. Stacpoole debars such sights, and reminds himself of the line he cannot cross by accusing nature, not his human characters, of decadence and corruption. Weeds in his view are 'voluptuous', and orchids are 'filthy-looking'. The adjectives seem excessive until you remember that flowers are the genital organs of plants: Stacpoole deflects criticism by castigating the amorality of the vegetable world. He is more lenient when describing planetary sex in the sky above the island. The old sailor who looks after the children during their early years explains dusk by improvising a myth about the male sun and its bawdy pursuit of its cool white female counterpart. 'He's gone chasin' the moon, an' she's skedadlin' wid her dress brailed up.' There is thus a precedent for Dick's adolescent wooing of Emmeline, which prompts Stacpoole to remark that 'she was his shadow and his slave. He was her sun'.

In stories like this, the geology and topography of the island determines what happens on it. Ballantyne differentiates between volcanic and coral islands. The former are made by a convulsion that spits out what Byron had called the lava of searing emotion. In his novel *Blown to Bits*, which ends with the eruption of Krakatoa, Ballantyne called the volcanic island 'an enormous hydro-electric engine', torn apart by the pressure of 'giant steam-jets'. The industrial metaphor is worthy of Jules Verne. But coral islands have a slower, stealthier genesis and suggest reveries of a more insidiously gloomy kind. They are many-storeyed boneyards, steadily built up by insects whose exoskeletons pile into a reef. Ariel in *The Tempest* tells Ferdinand that his father's bones are made of coral, but coral itself is bone from which the flesh has mouldered. After a hurricane battered a Samoan harbour in 1889, Robert Louis Stevenson imagined the capsized warships that had begun to rust in this 'place of sepulture', with human skeletons and metal hulls gripped by the tentacles of coral. *The Coral Island* overlooks these gruesome foundations, and emphasizes instead the devotion with which the self-sacrificing insects, like Gothic masons, build up their edifice: the knobbly texture of the cavern reminds Ralph of 'the fretwork of a noble cathedral'. He wonders how an island that seems to consist of glinting gems came to be formed but can 'arrive at no certain conclusion'; no doubt when back in England he acquired the information he needed by reading Darwin's analysis of coral. Crossing the Indian Ocean on *The Beagle*, Darwin visited the Keeling or Cocos Islands, which he defined as 'lagoon-islands (or atolls)'. He was fascinated by the way these 'sunken islands' kept their heads above water, forming a surface from lumps of coral regurgitated by the surf and flurries of wind-blown sand. So it was that life, in Darwin's theory of nature, sustained itself on a bedding of death. He had no interest in stories about the adventures of men or boys in such places, and concentrated instead on the island's struggle to exist. Do the holiday-makers in the Maldives realize that they are frolicking among what Darwin called 'upraised organic remains'?

This union of morbidity and fecundity appealed to Darwin, but what attracted Ballantyne and Stacpoole was coral's mediation – like a missing link – between different states of being. Ballantyne's boys initially compare the submarine shrubs of coral to 'the brain of a man', growing on stalk-like necks. Later, puzzled by the island's origins, they seem to be staring down into a mental abyss, and Ralph says that their thoughts about the reef are 'so

profound' that they risk drowning in them. Alive, the polyp's tip squeezes out
a sticky milk; when it dies it leaves behind a calcified deposit of limestone.
Is it vegetable or mineral? Stacpoole, who shared Darwin's fascination with
'the romance of coral', treats the atolls as organisms: like his adolescent
characters, they are forever 'secreting, excreting, and growing more highly
organized'. It amused Stacpoole that the polypifer, in truth 'a sluggish and
gelatinous worm', was held up to Victorian children as a model of efficient
workmanship. Ballantyne's boys call it a 'wonderful insect'. Ralph, Jack and
Peterkin are frivolous and shiftless; the Crusoe-esque diligence of the coral,
as it manufactures houses from calcareous traces in the water, may be some
compensation. Although Stacpoole mockingly denounces the polypifer as a
'hobo', it creates a barricade for his island, muffling the concussion of the surf
and reducing waves to a foam that resembles powdery 'white marble'; inside
that cordon lies his equivalent of the tank in Ballantyne's story – an unruffled
lagoon that connotes innocence because the colour blue is for Stacpoole
'seraphic', appropriate for the vestments of his two naked angels. The reef is
in a way a mental barrier, like the taboo inscribed on the beach. Where the
'savage' sea assails it, the surf thunders. But if you can find an opening, you
reach the becalmed lagoon, as uterine as Ballantyne's cave. When the boat
makes its way through the reef, Emmeline believes she is in what Stacpoole
calls Wonderland (though on J. M. Barrie's map it goes by the name of Never
Land). She and Dick arrive on what Stacpoole describes as 'the happy shore';
because the lagoon is 'a lake in the midst of the ocean', they might be embryos
afloat in Wordsworth's unborn Eden. The turbulent Pacific is, as Stacpoole
says, 'pacified by the reef'. Behind this buffer, art – which is life with the
leisure to reflect on itself – becomes possible. On a coral jetty by the reef, a
palm tree bends over, 'seeking its reflection in the waving water'. The lagoon
is the pool where Narcissus examines his identity and admires his beauty; it is
the mirror in which the first aesthetic replicas of reality form.

Like Crusoe educating Friday, the children offer to teach the illiterate old sailor how to sign his name (which they misspell), but he prefers not to learn. A name is a socially assigned label, useless on a desert island. If the long epic of human cultivation and improvement is not to be repeated, what happens instead? To place children on an unspoiled island might be a prescription for restaging the fall of man, but Stacpoole rules out this option. The breadfruit and coconuts they consume do not grow on a tree of knowledge; intellectual freedom is not demonized here as it is in Eden, because the children remain blissfully ignorant. Stacpoole renounces religion and imagines 'nature…in an experimental mood', studying how human organisms actually grow when the embargos that lour over the biblical garden are removed. The experiment is explicitly Darwinian. Stacpoole notices that Emmeline, a plain child, has 'evolved' into a 'perfectly formed…fully developed' young woman, and Dick's games are described as his 'evolutions on the sand'. In the biblical story, death is the penalty for disobeying God's law – and sexual guilt is one of the early symptoms of that moral lapse, which is why Adam and Eve only take to wearing fig leaves after their fall from grace. But in *The Blue Lagoon* death comes naturally, not as a dictatorial judgment, and it serves as an incitement to sex, because a world that is mortal needs to be replenished and renewed. The old sailor quietly expires on a ledge of coral, to which he might be contributing his own corpse. Larvae have already consumed one side of his face when the children find his body, and a live crab – its feast on his innards interrupted – darts from his gaping mouth. Christianity made death the gateway to eternal life; Darwinian science reversed the sequence by pointing out that life feeds on death.

Ballantyne's boys wisely choose to abandon the island; Stacpoole's characters are ejected from theirs. While swimming in the lagoon, Dick is threatened by a shark. He scrambles into the boat, but loses the paddle. Without it, he and Emmeline are washed out through the reef. The sea, as

Stacpoole puts it, takes the island from them: the process is involuntary, like maturation. Improbably enough, Dick's father who has spent the interim scouring the Pacific is on hand to rescue them, though this too is an alarming prospect: how will the wider world view what has happened to them? Just in time, condemnation is averted. Their boat contains some crimson berries that the sailor long ago warned them not to eat. But they are too hungry to resist, and they collapse into a coma from which, as the sailor predicted, they may never wake up. Dick's father asks if they are dead; he is told that they are sleeping. Their coma is at best a love-death, which painlessly saves them from the tragedy of repatriation to the adult, censorious American mainland.

A wreck is generally enough to get people onto the island they have secretly dreamed about. Indeed in romantic versions of the story, the wreck was – as Nietzsche said when deploring the nihilism of Wagner's operas – 'the goal, the secret intent, the true significance of the voyage'. To clamber alive onto the island, like Crusoe, was a dreary anticlimax, best avoided. In Barrie's view, birth was a shipwreck, which meant that we were all victims. The lucky few, however, could be saved from that fate. The wreck, in Barrie's stories about islands, is replaced by a rape – a seizure, a ravishment, which both physically and emotionally transports those to whom it happens, like the Darling children in *Peter Pan* when they are whirled off to Never Land.

Barrie tells the story in the customary way in his play *The Admirable Crichton*, where a shipwreck deposits a hapless aristocratic clan and its servants on a Pacific island. The butler Crichton, so obsequious at home, bossily rallies his incompetent employers and turns the world upside down. When two years later they all return to England, 'the other island', revolutionary misrule is suspended and Crichton slips back into servility. Peter Pan can stay on his island indefinitely, because he refuses to grow up. In another of Barrie's plays the reprieve from time follows a kind of death. In *Mary Rose*, a Hebridean island becomes an active, perhaps malignant agent. The islands of Ballantyne and Stacpoole harbour experiences that cannot be reconciled with grown-up normality, which makes them bashful, evasive places. In *The Blue Lagoon*, a breeze from the land makes a weak attempt to resist or repel the castaways; the island wants to remain inviolate. But the local people in *Mary Rose* say that their island 'likes to be visited'; the only problem is that those who visit it dematerialize. Opening onto another kind of annihilating Never Land, it seems eerily mystical, as if a Celtic holy island had been overtaken by a new religion. Two thin, stricken trees gesticulate in vain, 'no longer [able to] pray to their gods to carry them away'. The desolate area is silent, 'as still as an empty church'. Are those who vanish here, like Mary Rose, immortal or ghoulishly undead? The island has a sinister aestheticism, more disturbing than Stacpoole's mirror-like lagoon. Cramming a lake and a stream, hillocks and a glade into 'a miniature land' that measures just six acres, it seems 'curiously complete in itself'. The completeness is curious because the act of creation has been deliberately left incomplete: this picturesquely varied, amenable terrain might have been prepared for human occupants, but there are none. Art reproduces the world, and in the process eliminates life. To a geometrizing eye, like that of Plato when he designed Atlantis, such a deduction hardly matters. It neatly transforms the island into a microcosm, 'about the size' (as Mary Rose's husband says before she disappears) 'of the Round Pond'.

That circular pool is in Kensington Gardens, in West London, not far from the house in which Barrie lived. Elsewhere in the gardens is the more irregular lake called the Serpentine, containing a sanctuary known as Bird Island. In Barrie's private mythology, this was where human babies hatched from eggs before being distributed to the parents who fostered them. Barrie liked the idea that humanity might be converted to an oviparous species; this would spare us our traumatic, protesting passage through the tunnel that is

recapitulated in *The Coral Island*. Perhaps the island in *Mary Rose*, guarding
its compact little world inside a circular capsule, is an unhatched egg. At the
end of the third act of *Peter Pan*, water rises and engulfs the rock on which
Peter is lolling. He is prepared to drown, and expects death to be 'an awfully
big adventure', but he also provides for a possible future by carrying off two
eggs which he removes from a bird's nest. Ballantyne's boys are amused by
the sedate demeanour of the penguins that carry their eggs in 'a most convenient cavity...between the tail and the legs'. Peter balks at doing the same
and instead deposits them in a pirate's discarded hat, which he uses as a
lifeboat: it is a floating, navigable island, the incubator for new life. He saves
the eggs as a favour to the bird that laid them, not because he has any enthu-
siasm for reproduction, though he may have miscalculated in taking a pair.
D. H. Lawrence in his story 'The Man Who Loved Islands' describes a misanthrope who lives on a succession of islands, each smaller and more bleakly
solitary than the last. He would have found the hat in *Peter Pan* intolerably
crowded: 'an island,' as Lawrence says, 'is a nest which holds one egg, and one
only. This egg is the islander himself'. In 1925, two years before Lawrence's
story was published, F. Scott Fitzgerald made the associative leap from islands
to eggs in *The Great Gatsby*, describing two oval extrusions into Long Island
Sound, known as East Egg and West Egg (based respectively on Manhasset
and Great Neck). Fitzgerald notes that the metaphorical resemblance 'must
be a source of constant confusion to the gulls that fly overhead'. The image
alludes to the fresh unspoiled beginnings of America, but it also contains
a threatening preview of the future: eggs are fragile, and relations between
the inhabitants of these twin outcrops lead to spillage, waste, slaughter. Peter
Pan, by contrast, protects the eggs he takes with him to his island. If only
there were no need for germination to occur, if only the eggs could retract into
the body that expelled them. Could this be what Ballantyne's penguins
have in mind?

Barrie's imaginary island eliminates sex: Wendy is imported to mother the lost boys, not to be Peter's wife. Or at least it debars sex of the approved, connubial kind. The lost boys were actually a tribe of five brothers for whom Barrie was a doting honorary uncle, and with a combination of naivety and naughty innuendo he told them – in dedicating the play to them in 1928 – that he had 'made Peter Pan by rubbing the five of you violently together, as savages with two sticks produce a flame'. He surely knew that there was a sexual motive in this ardent friction. The savages in *The Coral Island* are enemies, cannibals who specialize in arcane torments; Barrie's joke incriminates himself. The aim of his fantasizing was to forestall puberty, which would reroute affection into new channels. Yet he blamed himself for hastening this change by publishing a story he and the boys had elaborated in the games they played together. 'One by one,' he wrote in the dedication, 'as you swung monkey-wise from branch to branch in the wood of make-believe you reached the tree of knowledge.' The monkeys are Darwinian, recalling Ballantyne's Peterkin who capers 'like a monkey'; the tree is biblical, and it tempts the boys with sexual awareness. The regretful remark is Barrie's complaint against the evolution of the species and the emotional growth of the individual.

As he admitted, his young companions did not share this infatuation with childhood. In 1901 he compiled an illustrated account of their summer revels, called *The Boy Castaways of Black Lake Island*. Black Lake was a turbid hollow in a Sussex pinewood, through which the brothers liked to wade; there was no island, except in their minds. The book recorded private enjoyments, which is why Barrie – avoiding the self-accusation that rankles in the dedication to *Peter Pan* – never published it. Only two copies were printed; he kept one, and gave the other to the boys' father. The first photographic plate shows one of the brothers shouldering an axe, while two more brandish gardening tools. The caption startlingly attributes a self-destructive agenda to them: they announce 'We set out to be wrecked'. The wreck, in Barrie's interpretation, was the unavoidable consequence of time, not the result of meteorological mischance as in *Robinson Crusoe* or *The Coral Island*. The boys in the photograph are armed for a career as colonists or cultivators, rather than being indigent castaways. Even Robert Louis Stevenson, the offspring of an engineering family, hesitated between treasuring his island as a nostalgic nursery and modernizing it by force. In 1893 in Samoa he joked about the mountain track that was 'the great public highway of the island', where travellers had to go single file. He fancied that the route was leading him to Lyonesse, the fabled kingdom of Arthurian legend that supposedly sank underwater off the Isles of Scilly; actually it conducted him on unromantic errands to the post office, and once at least brought him into contact with a bothersome tax inspector.

At the end of *Treasure Island*, Jim and his colleagues leave the three pirates behind. To disclaim or disperse responsibility, his account carefully employs passive verbs: 'A council was held, and it was decided to desert them on the island'. Can this be what a desert island actually is? – not a barren desert, nor even a refuge for deserters like Fletcher Christian, but a place that the righteous feel bound to desert? Stevenson was enraptured by the mythical making of the Polynesian islands, which were fished from the ocean by demigods like jewelled lumps of coral. Jim's judicious achievement, as he advances into law-abiding maturity, is to reverse the process, destroying rather than creating: 'Before noon, to my inexpressible joy, the highest rock of Treasure Island had sunk into the blue ocean.' He has awoken from a nightmare, and is growing up into something like the disillusionment of the adult Stevenson, who in 1891 remarked that 'the Pacific is absolutely desert' – as empty as eternity. The word is put to an even starker use in Stevenson's description of a German coconut plantation on Samoa that, with its fanatically regular alleys of trees, is 'a desert of food'.

11. CASTAWAYS OR OUTCASTS?

At the beginning of *Gulliver's Travels*, a map situates the undersized kingdom of Lilliput in the vicinity of Van Diemen's Land. I grew up with this kind of dismissive gesture: the bottom of the world was given over at best to monstrosity, at worst to absurdity. Tiny and trivial, how could we be taken seriously? Increasing familiarity did not rid the southern hemisphere of its deviant oddities. Before Darwin abandoned the idea of gods as makers, he toyed with the notion that the earth was stocked by two independent creators: the Bible accounted for nature above the equator, but Australian marsupials and eucalypts must have been the caprices of some other deity. For the nineteenth-century mind, the globe's upper and lower halves remained unbalanced, and to migrate from north to south was like moving from one cranial hemisphere to the other – from the strict logic of the left side to the instincts and impulses of the right.

Paul Gauguin fled to Polynesia in 1891 to escape from money-grubbing Christianity. Like Stevenson, he was delighted by myths in which the islands were fished out of the ocean: this meant that they were found, not made by a creator who – as in Eden – retained the right to supervise the behaviour of his creations. Even after he settled in Tahiti, Gauguin confessed that he could not cross 'the profound gulf which separates an Oceanian soul from a Latin soul'. The two souls clashed when Gauguin introduced his child-bride Tehura to the wife of a local gendarme. Carnal nature faced up to law and artifice, and the Frenchwoman's snooty contempt made Gauguin ashamed of his own race. Herman Melville contrasted the festooned peeresses in Westminster Abbey with the 'savage maidens' of Polynesia, dressed only in scanty skeins of flowers; he found the choice between a milliner's dummy and a pigmented Venus de Milo easy to make. Like Gauguin, Melville was an apostate – a runaway not a castaway. In 1842 he deserted a whaling vessel in the Marquesas and spent three weeks living with the natives, after which he joined another whaler and jumped ship again in Honolulu, criss-crossing the Pacific like a tramp in the Depression hopping on and off freight trains. Returning home after almost four years at sea, he wrote about cohabiting with cannibals in *Typee*. His account of his experience is at first unashamedly blissful. Gambolling in the water with native girls, he delights in the teasing of these 'river-nymphs', as if he were Odysseus romping with Calypso. He is infantilized by idleness, so his servant Kory-Kory is more a nurse than a valet: he bathes his wounded master after carrying him to a jungle pool, and spoons coconut, banana and roasted breadfruit into his mouth. Melville's daily routine blurs into an 'undiversified' sensual stupor, with meals punctuated by languid siestas. Life in the Marquesas, he reports, is 'an often interrupted and luxurious nap'. The island, like art, is a wish-fulfilling dream.

Melville deplored the militant conquest of what he called 'the evangelized islands', and saw Christian missionaries in the Pacific as agents of the same vengeful crusade that had 'extirpated Paganism from the greater part of the North American continent' by rounding up and killing off 'the greater portion of the Red race'. The Marquesans already had gods of their own, earthier than the abstractions worshipped in the other hemisphere. A naked warrior admired by Melville resembles a statue of Apollo – except that the fixed classical prototype is quickened into athletic life, and its marble pallor is overrun by a tattoo that makes the young man's back look like an espaliered vine on a garden wall. On another occasion Melville notices priests tenderly cradling a small inanimate idol, which he calls a 'baby-god'. Their need for such an object of worship demonstrates that these people, in the view of a worldly-wise modern man, have not advanced beyond childhood; but the phrase also acknowledges that babies everywhere are temporary gods, idolized by doting parents. The believer is bound to be disappointed when his prayers are not answered, and the local religion allows for a venting of grievances that Christianity prohibits. Watching as the worshippers chastise their idol and stuff it back in its box, Melville comes to pity the 'unfortunate deities' of the Typees. In the jungle he finds another battered, disregarded god carved from wood, now disintegrating into wet, mossy compost. The sufferings of 'his godship' are a credit to the islanders, who treat divinities with such gruff lack of reverence and throw them away when they have served their purpose.

Melville deplored the French invasion of the Marquesas, and questioned the benefits the northerners offered. If we judge civilization by its results, he suggested, 'it would perhaps seem better for what we call the barbarous part of the world to remain unchanged'. In 1893, summing up the brutal competition of German, British and American interests in Samoa, Robert Louis Stevenson went further: he accused the feuding empires of responsibility for the 'progressive decivilization' of the islands. The contradiction is cruelly pointed. Progress, the imported doctrine, was the enemy of civilization; a rooted, customary way of life was no longer protected by its insularity.

Stories about treasure islands told an unwitting truth. The European empires that squabbled over Polynesia during the nineteenth century wanted to plunder its wealth and open new markets for their own commodities. Treasure is loot, grubbed from the ground and expropriated, like the 'buried gold' that is a provocation to murder in Stevenson's story. This may be why Stevenson discouraged the curiosity and cupidity of his readers: when asked by journalists in Sydney about the location of his imaginary island, he evasively replied that it was not in the Pacific.

Treasure Island was published in 1883, six years before Stevenson settled in Samoa; it belongs to the decadent end of the century, not its glad youth, and the island is a sepulchral place where people fight over a grave containing gold. Nature here is literally reddened by human predators: after murdering one of his fellow sailors, Long John Silver cleans his bloody knife on the grass. When Jim Hawkins first sees the island, he shudders with revulsion at its moaning surf and melancholy woods. A metaphor explains its spiritual misery: the hills conclude in peaks, vertical tumuli that are 'wild stone spires', and the tallest of them, sliced off at the top, resembles 'a pedestal to put a statue on'. Or a pedestal, perhaps, from which a statue has been toppled. The spires point to an empty sky, with the gods on duty as sentinels. Decadence is decomposition, which explains the odour of decay given off by the sodden leaves and rotted tree trunks. The ship's doctor calls the place pestiferous, and warns of malaria; the medical diagnosis of the landscape has a particular grimness because Stevenson hoped that Samoa would be a sanatorium, soothing his weak lungs and arresting his 'slow dissolution'. Despite its promise of enrichment, the island is populated by corpses. A skeleton serves as a compass, and the blockhouse is a mortuary. The dead O'Brien leans against the bulwarks of the ship like a puppet; Jim, mastering his fear, grabs him like a sack of bran – death, as Darwin explained, is the nutriment of nature – and pitches him overboard, then watches as 'the quick fishes' gather for a feast.

When the treasure is exhumed, Jim marvels at its global diversity – 'English, French, Spanish, Portuguese, Georges, and Louises, doubloons

and double guineas and moidores and sequins', with a smattering of 'strange
Oriental pieces'. Stevenson's linguistic images devalue the insignia stamped
on the coins to establish their worth: the Arabic lettering, he says, looks like
'wisps of string or bits of spider's web'. Stevenson qualifies Jim's delight by pre-
senting him as an amateur numismatist. He derives pleasure from 'sorting' the
coins, and because he regards them as a 'collection' of curios he has no thought
of spending them. Another metaphor at once vouches for his good faith and
breezily discredits the hoard. Jim says that the coins are 'like autumn leaves':
he means that they are innumerable, which is a reminder that he is catalogu-
ing not counting them, but the remark also underlines the sterility of these
wind-blown trophies. Days of stooping over the spoils make his back ache,
and his fingers hurt from raking through the coins. Money has begun to turn
a boy into another expended cadaver, with bony digits reaching for a pile
of obsolete metal.

In our fantasies, as Freud pointed out, we always award ourselves untold
wealth (along with a supply of compliant sexual partners). Stevenson's stories
about South Sea islands expose the fallacy of these mercenary reveries. In
'The Bottle Imp', a genie promises a Hawaiian instant enrichment; in another
Hawaiian fable, 'The Isle of Voices', a sorcerer turns shells into dollars. The
island in this story is uninhabited, so the magical transformation shows up
the collaborative fiction of currency, which only has value if others agree
to recognize it as it circulates. The tribesmen are terrorized by a haunted
beach, where invisible speakers chatter in French, Dutch, Russian, Tamil
and Chinese. Caliban's noises, delightful and harmless, have now become
verbal, and they announce an end to the old peaceful pastoral life. Stevenson
says that the bewitched ground was 'as thick as a cried fair': the Pacific was
a market, and the devils are the polyglot usurpers who dispute control of it.
A local economy has no need of coinage, but there can be no international
trade without it: Kalamake in 'The Bottle Imp' uses his devilish dollars to

buy imported delicacies – tinned salmon, gin – from a trading ship that visits his island once a month. Because the monetary system is so artificial, credit and credibility drain from it. The imp's curse demands that the bottle be sold for less than the current owner paid for it, which means that transmission devalues it. Keawe panics because he bought it for a cent: how can he sell it at a loss? The Babel of currencies in the Pacific gives him his chance, if he slithers through the crevices between conversion rates. His wife insists that 'all the world is not American'. (At least it wasn't in 1891, when Stevenson published the story; Hawaii, however, was taken over as a United States territory in 1898.) She reminds Keawe that English farthings are worth half a cent, and suggests they speed to 'the French islands', because on Tahiti they can sell the bottle for a centime, which is worth only a fifth of a cent. Her fractions are an inverse profiteering, and they mock the acquisitive mania of capitalism.

In Joseph Conrad's story 'A Smile of Fortune', based on a voyage he made in 1888, a trader in Mauritius is duped into buying thirty tons of potatoes, which weigh on him like the spell of the bottle imp. Under duress he hauls them to Australia, where there is a potato famine; in Melbourne he offloads his cargo for three times the original price. Profits are a kind of magic – white or black? – and are conjured out of nothing like Mauritius itself, which rises from the water like 'a mere emanation' or an 'astral body'. Conrad is sarcastic about the local description of the island as 'the Pearl of the Ocean'. Pearls may be beautiful, but they also have a price attached, which taints them. The collusion between fantasy and commerce recurs in Stevenson's 'The Ebb-Tide', set on an island that is 'undiscovered' and 'scarce-believed in', so illusory that it has to be evoked by transparent, weightless metaphors. It is even likened to Laputa in *Gulliver's Travels*, an island that flies rather than floating. Perhaps it is an isle of the dead, because – as a character remarks with a superstitious shiver – its houses are empty and its graveyard full, while the islanders are referred to as 'souls', implying that they no longer possess bodies. There turns out to be a hard-headed reason for the island's elusiveness: speculators conspire to keep it off government charts in order to monopolize its pearls. The morass of *Treasure Island* is said to be unhealthy, but in 'The Ebb-Tide', Stevenson offers a more drastic diagnosis of the ailments that infest 'the island world of the Pacific'. The men of the European diaspora 'carry activity and disseminate disease': the comment neatly and justly equates commerce and contagion.

Stevenson was witnessing an accelerated rerun of social and economic changes that had taken centuries in the northern hemisphere. Hustled by European traders and the armies and engineering corps that cleared the way for them, Samoa was jolted in a few decades from 'a period of communism' to 'the age of finance', or from a ceremonious patriarchal regime to the competitive individualism of modernity. Despite his disquiet, Stevenson found himself participating in this enforced change. He belonged, as he told his friend Colvin, both to civilization and to barbarism; his house at Vailima was 'embowered in forest', yet he viewed the jungle as 'our strangling enemy...which we combat with axes and dollars'. Wielding a cutlass, he chopped his way through the bush, felling 'soft, sappy trees' that were vulnerable because of their sloth. He massacred the encroaching tuitui plant, then 'attacked the wild lime, and had a hand-to-hand skirmish with its spines and elastic suckers'. Plants turned into inanimate animals, which made the battle tougher. He described the proliferating weeds as reptiles, and said he was 'on the hot chase' of 'the rooted beast'. Dabbling in viscous slime, he accused himself of 'continual murders'. Gauguin had a similarly regressive experience on an expedition with the Tahitian woodcutter Totefa. The purpose was to find a certain kind of wood Gauguin wanted to carve; Totefa led him through a 'mad vegetation' of pandanus, hibiscus, guava and giant ferns, which grew denser as they forced a way into it, both of them naked and brandishing hatchets. Totefa went on ahead, with Gauguin admiring his sleek androgynous body. The young man looked to him like a continuation of the palpitating plant life that coiled around them:

while Stevenson promoted stubborn shrubs to mettlesome wild animals, Gauguin embedded Totefa in the dank, fertile ground from which he might have grown. As the two men drew closer to each other, fever made the painter's knees knock together – not malaria, as in *Treasure Island,* but a more alarming sexual excitement. Their joint attack on a rosewood tree relieved the tension. As his axe slashed the trunk, Gauguin thrilled to a spasm of 'divine brutality', as if he were performing surgery on 'the old civilization within me' – or perhaps cutting out the uncivilized desire he felt for Totefa. In 1893 Stevenson experienced a similar resurgence of primitive delight during preparations for a tribal war. He and a companion watched a chieftain perform a belligerent dance, hurling his knife in the air and catching it. 'The old aboriginal awoke in both of us,' Stevenson reported with a flush, 'and knickered like a stallion.'

The ritualized society of Samoa conferred a ceremonial function on Stevenson: he was known as Tusitala, the teller of tales – a tribal bard, the kind of communal historian for whom the hasty, forgetful societies of the northern hemisphere had no further use. But when he retold his tales for readers at home, he was unsure what genre to assign them to. Were these sagas about territorial disputes genuine epics or only desecrated parodies? He often likened the Samoans he knew to figures from the classical past: his cook resembled the Roman statue of a fighting gladiator, and a chief had the body of Homer's Ajax. Nor could he help recalling the bravado of Robert the Bruce and his highland warriors, resisting English incursions. Though he wanted to honour the battle for Samoa as 'a chivalrous war', he had to admit that its muddled conduct was often more like the 'mixed genus' of mock-epic or tragic farce. Cows grazed while the tribes exchanged gunfire around them; a pile of severed heads, trophies of combat, turned out to include one belonging to a harmless girl. The ruminating cows warned Stevenson that his tales were bound to end not in victory but in the resumption of somnolent, unhistorical routine. After the war, in gratitude for his role as their go-between with the new colonial administration, the chieftains teamed up to widen the track that led to his house. In a speech thanking them, he talked about the imperial road-building of the Romans, who also turned from fighting to digging and drove highways through marsh and bush. This rousing rhetorical tribute ignored an ultimate truth. Four years earlier, at the start of his campaign against the tuitui, he acknowledged that 'Rome perished' despite its virtues and skills, while the plant, with its tough root, feeble stem and indigestible seeds, would 'outlast the eternal city'. Islands are intractable; no matter how hard it tries, culture can never vanquish nature.

For Ballantyne and Barrie, childhood was an island, a state of grace where the disorienting lapse into puberty could be indefinitely postponed. Gauguin travelled in search of a more atavistic past: Polynesia, he said in 1895, exhibited 'the original source...the infancy of mankind'. Actually what interested him was the adolescence of mankind, represented by Tehura. The same fixation is the subject of *Rarahu*, a novel published in 1880 by a French naval officer who used the pseudonym of Pierre Loti. His shipmates teased him for his bashfulness by nicknaming him 'le Loti', after an Indian flower that shyly hid in the undergrowth; Loti had prudent reasons for concealment, and the child brides in his fiction – first the fourteen-year-old Maori girl Rarahu, then the underage geisha Madame Chrysanthème, a forebear of Puccini's Madama Butterfly – were a cover for the pubescent males on whom he actually doted. Loti tells Rarahu that Tahiti was regurgitated by the sea, and emerged red-hot; she perches on its summit, as if her body were the crater through which the volcanic fires express themselves. By contrast, the 'unknown islands' in 'distant seas' from which Loti comes are bound to founder, taking the white race with them. His contempt for what he calls 'our hateful civilization' is a baffled plea for liberation. E. C. S. Handy, who transcribed the legends of the Marquesas in the 1920s, reported that the islanders took a pleasingly aesthetic view of erotic matters. For them, sex meant 'sport, or play', rather than the dutiful procreative drill of the West. In her anthropological study *Coming of Age in Samoa*, Margaret Mead suggested that the hedonism of the local culture spared young people the neurotic anxiety that afflicted American adolescents. The region served as a geographical id, a zone of frank, unforbidden desire.

To work like Crusoe was to miss the point of residence in paradise. Gauguin reported that Tahiti lacked the monetary economy that corrupted Europe. The natives neither bought nor sold, because nature's gifts were shared by all. The only stock in trade of Loti's characters is bodily products: Rarahu's foster-father, having spent his life nurturing a white beard, sells it for its weight in gold. Loti smiles on the indolence of 'grown-up children' who do not need to wear themselves out earning their daily bread. He approves of Rarahu's indignant refusal to become an old-maid schoolteacher, and remarks that he loves her because she is so mentally docile. The business of her life is to bathe and wander through the woods, to dream and sing; like the decadent artists of the 1890s, she relishes each delicious instant as it passes. Loti, unable to quell his imported impatience, yawns when he contemplates 'the monotony of eternal summer', but the climate, stalling time in a balmy somnolent 'Oceanian noon', perpetuates pleasure. Sex here is not a seasonal activity, and the entire year can be spent in sensual dalliance. It is all so entrancing that a taboo has to intrude, warning the renegades that they have befriended people who violate the sanctity of human life: like Melville, Loti has a moral awakening that derives from his fear of cannibalism. The sailor in *Typee* realizes that he is being pampered to fatten him for a feast, and absconds in terror. Loti broods about the practice of anthropophagy because it transforms oral indulgence – which is the initial appeal of the islands – into an abomination. He winces when the queen of Bora-Bora shows off her portcullis of 'large cannibal teeth', and is alarmed by the 'huge square cannibal jaw' of the muscular chieftain Tamatoa. A Maori connoisseur tells him that the flesh of white men tastes like ripe, browning bananas. He is disgusted, but all the same likens his own taste for Rarahu to a fondness for 'fine fruit or fresh waters', as if she too were an edible titbit or a refreshing drink. Stevenson understood the reasons for this revulsion. Cannibalism, as he put it, 'unmortars a society', eroding the ligature of trust and respect that should bind us to the other members of our species. But he knew better than to fulminate about barbarous practices, as Melville and Loti do when they begin to feel guilty about their lives of glutted enjoyment; the islands schooled Stevenson in relativism, and he acknowledged that, in the eyes of vegetarians or Buddhists, carnivores like himself were no better than man-eaters.

Such qualms about cultural treason made departure inevitable. Gauguin returned temporarily to France after two years. He left Tehura weeping on the quay, her tiny feet dangling in soiled water, the flower she had worn in her hair wilting in her lap. Loti equates leave-taking with death, but it is Rarahu for whom it is terminal, after the dilettante sails off to have other adventures elsewhere. On the afternoon before his departure, the sun sinks with stealthy gradualness, warming the treetops as if for the last time; the sensitive plants, the tuitui so hated by Stevenson, retentively fold up their leaves. Tomorrow, he tells himself, both Tahiti and Rarahu will 'vanish like the scenery of an ended act in a play'. His metaphor defines the island as a painted set, and dispenses with the woman as a mere actress. Butterfly in Puccini's opera retires behind a decorative screen to disembowel herself; if Rarahu survives, it is not for long. A few years later in Malta, Loti is told that she consoled herself for his absence with the brandy bottle, which hastened the advance of the consumption that killed her. His novel ends with a prophetic nocturnal vision in which Cythera becomes an isle of the dead. Loti sees a black boat glide over stagnant waters and grind to a halt on a jagged coral beach. The sun rises, but it does so pallidly. Graves gape open, disclosing crabs that feed on corpses, and brittle bones reddened by the volcanic soil. The stark figure of Rarahu, bleached by death, lies on the sand. When he inspects the remains, her ghoulish face laughs at him, and the sun promptly expires in the chaotic sky. To punish himself for his moral truancy, Loti dreams up a last judgment that punishes his civilized crime and at the same time obliterates the earth.

The shared heat of sensuality does not protect Loti against a mortal chill, which makes him shiver when he thinks about Crusoe. With the wind wailing and the waves sobbing, he remembers his own forsaken situation, abandoned in an ocean that is the vastest of 'earthly immensities, stretching to the occult shores of the south-polar continent'. Surrounded by his adoptive family of Tahitians, Loti was never alone, but he suffered from what Joseph Conrad called 'moral solitude', an ailment peculiar to those who tried to lose themselves and efface the past in the yawning Pacific. A new kind of extra-territorial islander has appeared: the castaway is replaced by a shamed and guilt-ridden pariah like the corrupted clerk Willems who vacillates between 'the wastes of the Pacific' and 'the sunny solitudes of the Indian Ocean' in Conrad's novel *An Outcast of the Islands*. The narrator of Conrad's story 'A Smile of Fortune' regards the ostracized trader Jacobus and his daughter as victims of an honorary shipwreck. Expelled from contact with 'the rest of mankind', they behave as if Mauritius were a desert island. She cowers at home in a house that could be 'a cavern in a cliff', and when he goes to his office he might as well be scavenging for flotsam on the shore. Islands are a natural refuge for people who have forfeited their membership of a wider society. Stevenson had his own term for these peripheral figures: in his survey of drifters in the Marquesas, he classified them as 'people "on the beach"'. The expression ambiguously extends to cover those who are beached – randomly cast up like driftwood – and those retreat to the beach because they belong on the margins, where land itself dissipates into granules and prepares to be washed away.

Stevenson understood the makeshift, provisional nature of island communities. He did not make the bigoted mistake of considering the natives less than human; what they taught him – particularly in their religious observances – was that being human is a relative matter, involving adjustments on a vertical scale that slides up and down between superhuman and subhuman. In the north, men worry about the loss of status that could equate them with animals. In the south, they are more alarmed by the prospect of being overtaken and even cannibalized by spirits. Stevenson quotes a missionary and anthropologist whose study of Melanesia persuaded him that 'when a native says that he is a man, he means that he is a man and not a ghost, not that he is a man and not a beast'. Even on Treasure Island, these flimsy, permeable moral borders are crossed. The pirates camp in a steamy bog. A monster emerges from this marsh, and is likened to a monkey or a shaggy bear, though it runs 'manlike on two legs'. It turns out to be the marooned sailor Ben Gunn, who in only three years alone on the island has forfeited his human form. He represents the downward mutation, while with his wooden leg and his crutch, Long John Silver is a grotesque sketch of the other change. He has not quite shed the body as spirits do, but he is a prosthetic and posthuman man, all the more nimble and tenacious for having got rid of a limb. Darwin was intrigued by what he called 'insulated species', inbred oddities like the gargantuan tortoises of the Galápagos or the finches that evolved different traits because they could not fly from one island to the other. Ben Gunn and Long John Silver look like specimens of the same kind, exceptions to the human norm. Ben recovers his humanity once he exchanges berries and oysters for a 'Christian diet': his salvation is some toasted cheese. At the other end of the taxonomic ladder, Long John speeds away as if mechanized, escaping retribution. Verne's mysterious island stretches the definition of humanity along the same extended scale. The domesticated ape Jup is a castaway who reverted to wildness after only a few months;

if he is a predecessor of homo sapiens, the engineers who industrialize the island graduate beyond humanity, since technology awards them a godlike control of nature.

Islands can function as laboratories: inside secure perimeters, alternative models of society are put to the test – hence Utopia, or a penal dystopia like Van Diemen's Land. After Darwin, the stories about experimental islands turned from political theorizing to biological tinkering. Are we right to think that ape and angel, bestiality and beauty have nothing in common? The two come embarrassingly close on Skull Island, an obscure and foggy enclave in the Pacific, where a virile gorilla abridges the species by developing a fixation on a young blonde woman, who responds to his lovesick advances by screaming; captured and taken to the island of Manhattan, King Kong scales the Empire State Building as if he were clambering up an evolutionary ladder. In a more recent fantasy, genetic engineering revives species that are mercifully extinct. On Isla Nubar near Costa Rica, cloned dinosaurs and swooping raptors frolic in the playground that an addled scientist calls Jurassic Park.

The first of these fables about rearrangements to the chain of being takes place on a nameless island off the coast of Peru, where H. G. Wells's mad vivisectionist Dr Moreau produces a menagerie of freaks, surgical hybrids of human and animal. Romantic tales imagined islands that wandered, as the Galápagos were reputed to do; the narrator in *The Island of Dr Moreau*, horrified by the miscegenated monsters that roam in the jungle, recoils from 'the unspeakable aimlessness of things upon the island', as if life itself were wandering in a futile circle, its onward evolutionary march blocked or reduced to a chancy course of trial and error. Moreau's island has a fuming crater and sulphurous hot springs which – as recessive as the swamp in *Treasure Island* – ventilate the 'charge of explosive animalism' concealed beneath the surface. Bogged down, sliding backwards, the hunted narrator of Wells's story cannot repeat Crusoe's civilizing achievements. He defines himself as an 'unhandy' man, who is incapable of making a pot (and in any case the island has no clay for him to work with). When Moreau's brutes set fire to a boat, he accuses them of maliciously frustrating his 'return to mankind'. But is he right to think that mankind is at home on the normative mainland? What he sees, when he surveys Moreau's bloody clinic, is 'human life in miniature', just as Darwin described the Galápagos as 'a little world within itself'. The view makes him despair: 'I lost faith in the sanity of the world when I saw it suffering the painful disorder of this island'. The final curse of Moreau's helper, butchered by the 'beast folk', extends even further. He declares life to be a mess, and says he is glad to be rid of 'this silly universe'. The adjective is startling but exactly right: it originally meant feeble or insignificant rather than foolish, so the remark writes off the universe as a botched job, like one of Moreau's surgical ventures. The gulf of space is as vacuous as the Pacific, and the planets scattered in it are idiotic, anomalous islands.

12. 'THERE'S ANOTHER ISLAND'

Darwin considered the Galápagos archipelago to be 'a group of satellites', all 'attached to America' despite the intervening 'open space of ocean, between 500 and 600 miles in width'. The image inevitably makes us think of outer space, where moons sycophantically orbit larger planets. But the word's origins are uncelestial: a satellite was at first a minion placed on stand-by, awaiting orders. Are islands – as I always suspected when growing up on mine – mere attendants, deferential lookers-on? In our interdependent world, such places can survive only by joining commercial empires and consenting to political alignment, like satellite dishes receiving orders from the ether. Otherwise they exist outside history, biologically unviable as Darwin suspected, and economically absurd. In 1826 the laird of the Hebridean island of Rum shipped its entire population of four hundred across the ocean to Nova Scotia, and replaced his human dependents with a cheaper, less troublesome flock of sheep. Rum remained unpeopled until 1845, when the Marquis of Salisbury bought it and turned it into a shooting estate, stocked with red deer whose only purpose was to be killed. The island of Sark, near Guernsey in the English Channel, was still governed feudally until 2008, and holds modernity at bay by banning all motor vehicles except tractors.

Islands like these encourage a guilt-ridden nostalgia: it is a comfort to know that our collectivized, speeded-up present contains relics of a simpler, slower past, when remote corners of the earth were not yet in constant electronic contact with the centre. In 1934 the film-maker Robert Flaherty documented the stubborn, stoical way of life on the Aran Islands off the west coast of Ireland. *Man of Aran* exhibits a grimly rudimentary culture, where people do for themselves what God in Genesis should have taken care of when laying the groundwork for human existence: their dogged, repetitive occupation is what they call 'making the land'. On jagged rocks, they create starveling farms by breaking the limestone with mallets, hauling kelp from the shore and mixing it with scavenged gobbets of clay; with luck, the powdery bedding can sustain a crop of potatoes. Crusoe had to improvise because he was a man alone. Flaherty shows an entire community obeying the same self-reliant edict. The men and women of Aran sew clothes from animal skins, render sharks' livers to provide oil, and repair their boats with scraps of cloth and tarred paper. The spectacle has a tragic primitivism, reminding us that our tenure on earth is hard-won. The islanders arduously secure the means of life, and defy a God whose providence does not extend this far offshore. Flaherty's commentary announces that the struggle will continue until the man of Aran ends his days 'or meets his master – the sea'. There can be no meeting with a maker, because man himself makes the land; instead the force that possesses mastery is a ruthless element.

Shortly before Flaherty paid tribute to the resilient people of Aran, the islanders on St Kilda, off the west coast of Scotland, accepted defeat. By 1930 the population had been reduced to thirty-six; in the absence of medical help, cases of influenza or appendicitis were fatal. When their crops had failed, the islanders petitioned the laird to remove them to the mainland; they must have found their new lives disorienting, since although they had never seen a tree on their wind-flayed clump of rock, many of them were put to work as foresters. Michael Powell, after reading about the evacuation of St Kilda, restaged it on Foula in the Shetland Islands in *The Edge of the World*, made in 1936. The island was still inhabited at the time, but it looked too denuded to be properly picturesque. Shetland ponies had been outlawed because they gorged on the scarce grass; Powell, judging them to be an indispensable part of the scenery, had to import a few. The mood of his film is elegiac, regretting a way of life lost to modernity. While the men of Aran merely subsist, the characters in *The Edge of the World* have the leisure for chivalric contests, demonstrations of their gallant unworldly idealism. Two young men resolve a dispute by competing to scale a dangerous cliff without using ropes, and an old crofter loses his life scrambling down another sheer cliff in quest of an auk's precious, pigmented egg. The restless hero Robbie migrates to Aberdeen, but refuses to work on a trawler: he has an antiquated snobbery about industrialized fishing. In a prologue, Powell admits the self-indulgence of his dilettantish attitude to Foula: he plays an urbane yachtsman cruising past the abandoned island who insists on going ashore and – as if out stalking on his private estate – immediately makes a contribution to its deathly desertion by shooting down a hawk. Even before they troop onto a steamer with their bundled belongings at the end of the film, the islanders have faded from view. Inside the stone church, the congregation chants a psalm about being led beside the quiet waters; the camera turns away from them to survey the ruffled fields, the shivering pools, and the stalwart barricade of cliffs.

The time he spent on Foula convinced Powell that the territories we cherish, like his beloved home county of Kent, are at once insignificant and irreplaceable. 'Are not all our continents islands,' he wondered in the book he wrote about making *The Edge of the World*, 'does not the great sea surround them all, and is not the whole multi-coloured world a drop in the ocean to

Somebody?' Although he valued the island's separateness, he could not forget the tribulations of the continent, riven by a political crisis. In the same year Auden made his journey to Iceland, where he hoped to find a pleasingly cranky unreality. But there was no escaping the anxieties of the present: having been nominated by the Nazis as the homeland of Teutonic virtue, Iceland was aswarm with Germans planning its incorporation into the Reich, and Auden uncomfortably rubbed shoulders with Goering's brother. Powell likewise found on Foula a farcical replica of the conflict that was convulsing Europe, and described a scrap between sheepdogs as 'one of the finest mixed fights ever seen outside a totalitarian state'. A remedy for such bellicose brawling also lay at hand: Powell wished that Hitler, Stalin and Mussolini could be rounded up and brought to Foula to be disciplined by his assistant John Seabourne, a former sergeant in the Royal Garrison Artillery who was more than a match for that trio of gangsters. But a film set is also a despotic regime, and Powell himself, as he joked, was the mad tyrant of Foula, commandeering battalions of men and flocks of sheep and issuing futile orders to the skittish weather, which blew a gale and marooned his crew for several weeks. An island is a playpen for the uncontrolled directorial ego, or – like Elba and St Helena – an open prison for a deposed dictator.

The world war rehearsed on Foula by Powell and his colleagues reinforced the links between continents and islands. The Japanese and the Americans fought tenaciously for control of the Solomon Islands or Guadalcanal, which were stepping-stones in the Pacific; the prolonged and exhausting campaign rid such places of the seductive appeal they possessed for travellers in the late nineteenth century. James Michener, a naval lieutenant stationed between 1942 and 1944 at Espíritu Santo in what was then called the New Hebrides, saw a landscape warped by the anxiety of men who had spent too many months waiting for battle to begin. In his *Tales of the South Pacific* he calls the island of Funafuti 'truly dismal', is disgusted by leprous, malarial Vanicoro, and says that Espíritu Santo itself, its trees seething with parasites, is 'grotesque, crawling'. This is not so much the pathetic fallacy as the pathological fallacy. Savo earns a pained compliment when Michener calls it 'that tragic island': here the Japanese sank four cruisers, killing more than a thousand American and Australian troops. When asked later about the Pacific, Michener summed up his military service as two penitential years spent on a rock, during which he suffered from mosquito bites, heat itch and fungus of the feet. His frustration is transmitted to the *Tales*, which are short stories, sometimes overlapping but mostly restricted to solitary characters and insignificant happenings: his book has the same shape as an archipelago.

Unlike Gauguin or Loti in Tahiti, Michener and his fellow recruits did not luxuriate in idleness. To be what they called 'island-happy' or 'rock-jolly' meant that they had been crazed by entrapment and ennui; the remedy, for those who could hitch a ride on military planes, was a spell in Australia, which Michener enviously calls 'that mighty island' – mighty because larger than those pyramidal piles of sweltering, insect-infested sand in the dreary ocean. Many of the stories take a vengeful pleasure in recalling how the construction battalions (nicknamed Seabees) mashed and flattened this hated terrain in preparation for combat. On Norfolk Island they sacrifice a monumental avenue of pines to clear room for an airstrip. At Konora in Indonesia, they bulldoze the jungle in a fortnight, knocking hills sideways to fill up ravines. Living coral is dredged from the lagoon by steel maws, manhandled by a steam shovel, then transformed into a substitute for cement; in the process it loses its jewelled allure. An officer shows Michener the crushed flowers of bone: the red coral looks bloody to him, and the whiter branches are ash-coloured, stricken. He remarks on the 'evil-smelling' milk the coral exudes, and shudders at its 'suction cups like those on the tentacles of an octopus' – buds that will now never grow. After aeons of effort, this organism raised the island; its labour is

briskly finalized by the Seabees, who dump the filler, roll it flat, and prepare
a tarmac from which bombers can take off. Mobilization is eagerly awaited,
because it promises departure. The islands look beautiful, as Michener rue-
fully acknowledges, only from the air.

There is an exception: there has to be one, to preserve our doting dream.
One of Michener's characters joins an expedition to sickly, brooding Vanicoro.
On the way, he is startled when the dawn mists dry up, and he calls out
'There's another island!' The discovery is so momentous, so precious in its contradiction of the pervasive gloom, that Michener's narrator repeats it: 'There
was another island!' Lieutenant Cable has sighted Bali-ha'i, which coyly hides
behind pearly humidity. Small enough to be 'perceived in one loving glance',
its form is invitingly anthropomorphic, and it seems 'to curve…like a woman'.
This is the harem where the French planters have secreted their womenfolk to
keep them safe from the lecherous American troops; Cable surveys a 'frieze of
women', as profuse and lush as the fruits they handle, who might be 'models
awaiting the immortalizing brush of Gauguin'. Offered his choice, he selects
Liat, 'a lovely statuette in brown marble'. The references to sculpture and painting are cautionary: the erotic seeks an alibi in the aesthetic, as if the under-age
prize were being carved not caressed, immortalized not impregnated. When
Rodgers and Hammerstein musically paraphrased Cable's cry in *South Pacific*,
they had Bloody Mary – the Tonkinese harridan who trades her daughter Liat
to the Marine from Philadelphia – candidly explain that Bali-ha'i is a floating
bordello. She begins by summarizing the distance between north and south:

> Mos' people live on a lonely island,
> Lost in de middle of a foggy sea.
> Mos' people long fo' anudder island
> One where dey know dey would lak to be.

In Hammerstein's libretto, she customizes the fantasy by telling Cable that 'Bali-ha'i mean "I am your special Island"…mean "Here am I"'. It is, in another possible translation, a wish immediately fulfilled by imagination. Does it belong in a war zone, or is it a flushed illusion, seen through the lurid purple and orange filters that tint it in Joshua Logan's film? The Pacific was littered with isles of the dead: on Iwo Jima, a stretch of volcanic rock only five miles long, thirty thousand American and Japanese soldiers managed to kill each other in a single month. To make the ordeal endurable, there had to be an outpost of Cythera in the vicinity.

Powell imagined corralling the European dictators on Foula, where geographical disputes might be settled in bouts of fisticuffs. In 1968 John Boorman retroactively simplified the war in the Pacific by stranding an American and a Japanese soldier on a rugged, entangled island where, deprived of weapons and forced to fall back on mental cunning, they struggle for supremacy. *Hell in the Pacific* was filmed in the Palau Islands, between New Guinea and the Philippines; Lee Marvin plays the cowboy and Toshiro Mifune is the samurai. The location turns the global conflict back into a boys' game of hide and seek, ridiculing the childishness of war. The combatants throw stones at one another, and Marvin pisses on Mifune from high above. Marvin, briefly dominant, throws spars of wood into the surf and sends Mifune to fetch them like an obsequious dog. But the roles can be reversed: are they antagonists or playmates, like Crusoe and Friday when they exchange positions in Tournier's novel? Even a war game requires a collaborative spirit, as the national teams must agree the rules of engagement. Because the setting renders conflict pointless, the only feasible activity is aesthetic. Mifune rigs up a wind chime made of shells threaded on a vine, which serves as an early-warning system to alert him to Marvin's presence; later, more disinterestedly, he carves a flute from bamboo. Marvin makes his own cacophonous American music by banging together his empty water canteen and his mug while tunelessly bawling hymns. The purest, most peaceable act of creation occurs when Mifune stakes out a Zen garden on the beach, using a rake of sharpened bamboo to trace the furrows of a dry ocean and setting rocks at intervals to stand for volcanic islands. He is rightly furious when Marvin – who has been amusing himself by retarding the advance of some sand crabs, as if playing with a flea circus – tramples his contemplative enclosure. After much inconclusive skirmishing, Marvin and Mifune realize that they will both die unless they make common cause; together they build a raft, though they are still squabbling in languages they do not share as they try to propel it through the reef.

There is an unexpected prescience in Boorman's plot. Marvin lunges at a tank of rainwater Mifune has collected, and is driven away. Rather than share his supply with an enemy, Mifune spites himself by destroying the canvas reservoir. When Marvin disappears into the jungle, Mifune smokes him out, rendering the air unbreathable. They are competing for resources, not territory: the earth is a finite island, and may in the end be as inhospitable as the insular boulders that Mifune places in the arid sand.

The American occupation after 1945 finally put an end to Japan's self-enclosure. Until the arrival of Commodore Perry's gunboats in the mid-nineteenth century, foreigners had been excluded from the country; now it was coaxed to reproduce the political economy of its conqueror. But a remote, forgotten island acted as a brake on the hectic progress of the new Japan, and demonstrated that modernity makes little difference to the elemental human lot. In 1960 Kaneto Shindo filmed *The Naked Island* on the Setonaikai archipelago in the Inland Sea. Like *Man of Aran* or the tuna-fishing episode in Rossellini's *Stromboli*, it is almost a documentary, because the island's physical limitations and the dull round of its subsistence economy allow no leisure for storytelling or for flights into fiction. Adventures are advents, interruptions of routine (which may mean that what happens on Lisca Bianca in Antonioni's film is, after all, adventurous). But *The Naked Island* restricts itself to studying the routine of a husband and wife who tend crops on their desiccated hillside farm with water brought in from the mainland several times a day, and – as on Aran – collect seaweed for use as manure.

Their island is neither primitive nor cast away. An aerial view at the beginning of the film shows the archipelago's conical hills, shaved and terraced for crops, with wild growth confined to crevices or impractical summits. But the absence of one vital resource turns the island into a desert, mocked by the expanse of audibly lapping, slurping water that surrounds it. The labour of the husband and wife is Sisyphean: they ferry fresh water across the salt water in buckets balanced on a bamboo pole, then carry it up a dusty hill on a twisting track with no secure footholds. They mutely concentrate on not spilling a drop; the only moment of intimacy between them comes after she stumbles and lets some water slop out of one her buckets, which prompts him to stride down the hill and slap her face, knocking her over. When one of their two children suddenly, inexplicably dies, despair provokes a wanton misuse of water. Losing control, the wife upturns a full bucket onto the plants, instead of feeding them with a trickle from the can. Then she pulls the miserable, thirsty crops out by the roots. This time her husband does not reprove her. She falls over sobbing and crawls across the cracked earth, toppled by grief. He watches her for a moment, then carries on working. After a while, so does she. Tragedy is an error of perspective.

The nakedness here is metaphorical: we are watching unaccommodated man and woman battling through life. The film is virtually silent, because the characters have nothing to say to each other and no wish to fritter away energy in saying it. The first utterance comes after almost an hour, as the father congratulates his son for catching a fat, valuable fish. 'Heave-ho!' he says, which is hardly conversation. The only action is arduous, repetitive, ritualized toil. The film painstakingly studies things that would usually be overlooked

– a boat's oar slicing the water as the wife steers it over the channel; a kettle boiling on an open fire; a goat munching leaves; water dribbling onto rows of identical plants. Kaneto Shindo's minimalism reduces art to a condition of austere simplicity that tests our distracted, jittery minds. To watch the film is to confront, for a short while, the mental challenge that toughened Crusoe and weakened Conrad's Decoud. Life on an island can enlighten us, or drive us mad.

Global commerce views every populated crumb in the ocean as a potential delivery address. How better for this all-pervasive economy to show off its munificence than by raining down packages on an uninhabited island? This bounty tumbles from the sky in *Cast Away*, directed by Robert Zemeckis and released in 2000; it does so by accident, because a Federal Express cargo plane has crashed in the Pacific, but the disaster turns out to be providential, and it warns that the disconnected freedom of islands is at an end.

Tom Hanks plays a FedEx systems analyst who survives the crash and takes delivery of the packages when they are washed up by the surf onto a beach in Monuriki, near Fiji. His character is called Chuck Noland: he is not an adaptable nonentity, like Odysseus when he renames himself Nemo or Noman, but a man who belongs to no land in particular, a deterritorialized ambassador for free trade and cybernetic shopping. He has been teaching American production-line methods to blundering Russians after the collapse of the USSR, but he views his own country as sceptically as any other, and he remarks, as he travels back to Memphis for Christmas, that the Russians deliver as slowly as the US postal service. His loyalty is to his multinational corporation, which enwraps the world in its convivial embrace. At home for the holiday, he watches a news flash on CNN – another synonym, like FedEx, for global omnipresence and the blessings of consumerism – which reports that Santa Claus has been declared fit to fly and has set off to shower presents on children in Bosnia. Noland himself departs for the Pacific on Christmas Day; FedEx, sending him flotsam from the downed plane, proves to be as bounteous as Santa. At first these donations seem to be a sardonic joke, deriding a culture of luxury where necessities are no longer provided. One package contains a pair of ice skates, an odd, unseasonal gift to send to someone in the southern hemisphere, where Christmas occurs in midsummer, but such superfluity fuels the affluent economy. Ice is one of the few civilized benefits that the marooned Noland misses: flying back to America after his rescue, he beams at the taste of an iced soda, and he praises ice again in a later scene while drinking a whisky. Until the 1870s, when factories for making ice were established in the East Indies, sweltering colonists had to ship it in from Boston. In the tropics, refrigeration was the proud symbol of an imported Western culture that cancelled the inconveniences of nature. Noland can hardly go skating on his tropical island, but he refuses to let the skates mock him, like the unspendable gold coins that tantalize Crusoe: he redefines the blades as knives and uses them to chop open coconuts, and the laces secure bandages that he ties around his wounds.

Noland gets through his psychological ordeal because commodities replace companions. Crusoe erases the memory of his drowned shipmates by remarking that he 'never saw them afterwards, or any sign of them, except three of their hats, one cap, and two shoes that were not fellows'. The glimpse of the mismatched shoes painfully releases the emotion he wants to repress: nothing is harder, after the death of a loved one, than disposing of their apparel. Noland, however, nonchalantly recycles the footwear of a dead colleague, and when he finds that the shoes he has removed from a corpse are too small for his torn, bleeding feet, he cuts out the toes and wears them as sandals. He is a Crusoe who never has a visitor, but he can do without Friday because he has Wilson: another FedEx package contains a beach volleyball that becomes his plaything and his playmate, its brand name serving as a personal identity. He anthropomorphizes the rubber blob, sketching a face with his bloody palm print and adding some scratches to demarcate eyes and a mouth. Wilson is expected to empathize: Noland hurls the ball away in a rage when, during a one-way conversation, his imaginary confidant does not support his plan to escape on a raft. He soon regrets the tiff, and after finding Wilson he touches up his facial image, again using blood as pigment. The relationship ends in tears. Wilson is eventually swept off the raft as it lurches through the reef into open sea; Noland sobs more inconsolably than he did for the fiancée he left behind.

Cast Away comes dangerously close to satirizing our dependence on the toys and gadgets we are told we must covet; it makes amends for this sourness by treating life on the island as a course in self-improvement. Noland arrives there chubby and unfit. After a lapse in time, we see him spearing fish in the surf and showing off a newly lean and taut body. Gratification seems to have happened instantly, although in fact the production closed down for several months while Hanks returned from Fiji to California to develop this honed physique. The narratives clash, but their contradiction exposes our snarled, contradictory motives as consumers. In one story, the man on the island gormandizes, ripping open parcels and celebrating Christmas every day of the year. In the other, he scourges this acquisitiveness and sweats off excess flesh in workouts that duplicate the hard physical labour from which our pampered society spares us. The island is at once a glutted supermarket and a purgative gymnasium. Back in Memphis after his rescue, Noland is unable to resume his gregarious social life. He goes off alone to Texas to deliver the last of the packages from the crashed plane, then considers his options. At a crossroads, he contemplates four routes that lead towards California, Canada and all other points of the compass; as the film inconclusively ends, he prepares to cast himself away again in this empty America of dust and scrub or – if he chooses the polar options – of white, abstract ice. His time as a castaway has taught him that nowhere is home, and that no land can ever truly belong to us.

13. 'THERE IS NO ISLAND'

In the epigraph to *Friday*, Michel Tournier explains the perennial appeal of Crusoe's story by quoting the critic Jean Guéhenno, who in the course of an essay on the vexed relations between Prospero and Caliban enigmatically remarks: 'There is always an island'. Like Guéhenno, Tournier takes it for granted that the island, being an archetype, will outlast the owners who compete for possession of it or bequeath it to their successors; it exists because we believe in it, even if it appears on no map. A different and perhaps timelier mantra is voiced in *The Island*, Michael Bay's recent science-fiction film about the perils of genetic engineering. In a subterranean clinic, clones bred as organ donors are kept in reserve until their originals – wealthy dwellers in the world above ground, which is a scorched and rusted post-industrial wilderness – need to replace a body part. As the clones apathetically shuffle through their trapped lives in an antiseptic catacomb, they are cheered up by being shown the usual blandly anthological images of white beaches, nodding palms and lapping waves. Every so often, one of them is selected by lot for a voyage to this spurious island. The lucky winner is treated to a festive send-off, then taken away to be secretly slaughtered so that his or her eyes or heart or kidneys can be transplanted to an ailing sponsor. The technician responsible for programming the escapist illusion eventually reveals the truth, and admits 'There is no island'.

That mournful phrase echoes beyond the film. Redundancy long ago began to threaten islands. When fishing and agriculture failed, the Isle of Man and the Channel Islands off the shores of Britain were relaunched as tax havens, resorts for non-resident capital. Even so, insularity has proved to be inconvenient. There is currently a scheme to resurrect the land bridge that connected Jersey to France in the last Ice Age: the plans sketch a sixteen-mile causeway that would incorporate a wind farm and tidal energy turbines, together with the fuel pipelines and fibre-optic cables that are the circulation systems of our interconnected world. Such technological tinkering would not help islands doomed by climate change. In April 2007, *Time* reported that the population of the Carteret Islands off New Guinea had been moved to higher ground before the ocean engulfed their homes. In the same month, the *New York Times* mentioned the submergence of some delta islands known as the Sundarbans, which crumbled when rivers decanted water from the melting Himalayas into the Bay of Bengal, displacing six hundred families and expelling the Bengal tiger from its habitat. Channels in the Finnish archipelago off Turku are silting up, which suggests that in time the sprinkled islands, with their red cabins, pebbly coves and squadrons of dragonflies, will rejoin the continent. Richard Branson is an owner of islands who knows that islands may one day be extinct. He is convinced that Greenland will sooner or later thaw, and has said that 'it is in the self-interest of all the islands on the earth to set an example', because they will be the first places to go under. Islands of the earth, unite: it might be a billionaire's paraphrase of the *Communist Manifesto*. Branson has an emergency plan for Necker and Moskito, his personal fiefdom in the British Virgin Islands. He plans to rid them of fossil fuels, harnessing energy from sun, wind and tides to power his battery of appliances. Islands, following the example of Atlantis, are laboratories in which such right-minded experiments can be conducted. The few thousand inhabitants of Samsø in the North Sea have weaned themselves off electricity imported from the Danish mainland, and now generate power with wind turbines or by burning straw and wood chip from trees that have toppled of their own accord. But principled housekeeping like this can only happen on a small, insular scale, and is unlikely to halt the liquefying of the poles.

Remorse makes us value what we have destroyed or discarded: geopolitically, islands are once again an attractive proposition. The more homogenized and borderless the world becomes, the more we regret the loss of an individuality that the nation state once protected. The imagination enjoys picking apart the overstretched agglomeration we call Europe, wondering what it would be like if the continent fragmented into an archipelago. In his fable *The Stone Raft*, José Saramago follows the unmoored travels of the Iberian peninsula, which spontaneously breaks off, drifts out into the Atlantic and, after narrowly avoiding a collision with the islands of the Azores, settles into place in mid-ocean like a buoyant Atlantis. This schism is an ancient Lusitanian dream: in *The Lusíads*, Vasco da Gama describes Iberia as a virtual island, and calls it the head of Europe – although the Portuguese now more often refer to the western extremity they occupy as the continent's arse-end. For much of the twentieth century, until the end of Salazar's regime in Portugal and Franco's in Spain, Iberia was insulated by its illiberal, xenophobic politics. Did membership of the European Union really put a stop to this isolation? Victor Hugo, metaphorically joining the Channel Islands to France, called them chicks that had strayed from the supervision of the mother hen. Likewise Saramago describes Europe as 'a loving mother', saddened by the mishap that ruptures the Pyrenees and sets Iberia adrift. But his allegorical flourish mocks the pretence that Europe is a family. Its members disagree, so why shouldn't it be dismembered? We conventionally personify states as ships, yet we expect

the ship of state to be permanently at anchor. Even when the runaway peninsula nears the American coast, legislators in Brussels insist that no communal
agreements have been jeopardized. As they hasten to point out, the separation
is minimal when compared with the mental gap between the British Isles and
the continent. One of Saramago's characters, impressed by the mixers that
churn cement to fill up the fissure in the Pyrenees, argues that the best way to
preserve Venice would be to weld the hundred islands together or to drain the
lagoon, as the Dutch did with their lowlands.

Islands are annoying because of the wasted space around them: the
reclamation of land at Battery Park City in New York or in Hong Kong and
Macao suggests that if we knew how to pave over rivers and seas and build
on them we might do so. Saramago's fantasy tells a more disorienting truth.
The earth rotates in space like the cement mixer, and the ground moves
beneath our feet; everything in our world is unfixed, provisional. But we
dare not admit this fluidity, which is why the peninsula's secession provokes
such metaphysical bewilderment. The politicians pretend that the raft of
granite is navigating with a purpose; they indignantly deny the possibility
of continental drift, which is outrageous because unteleological. The people
on the sea-going peninsula see things differently, according to the law of
contrary motion. They seem to be at rest, and cannot understand why other
supposedly solid, rooted landmasses are speeding through the water towards
them. Lisbon waits for the Azores to loom up and ram into it: the islands are
projectiles aimed at the continent, not projections of the continent that have
fallen off and wandered away.

Perhaps Saramago should have exercised the magic realist's rights and
made the errant peninsula crumble into another fractious archipelago. His
characters expect the Algarve to secede, because it has always thought of
itself as a Moorish kingdom properly belonging to North Africa; the Spanish
region of Galicia would prefer to belong to Portugal, whose language it shares,

and Catalonia and the Basque country also dislike being forcibly glued to
Spain. Only the lack of tectonic friction keeps the shaky compound together.
But at least Iberia's new mid-Atlantic location preserves its independence:
this, in Saramago's view, is preferable to the prospect of European federation,
which would turn every country from Finland to Portugal into a facsimile
of Switzerland – though what is Switzerland but a set of alpine islands raised
high above sea level, with autonomous communities of French, German and
Italian speakers clustered in the foothills?

The burgeoning of extra islands is a happy idea; so is the notion that an
island might be as navigable as a yacht, smoothly transporting you wherever
you fancy. The opposite prospect is more bleakly terminal. In 2005 in *The
Possibility of an Island*, Michel Houellebecq foresees a future when the world
will no longer be divided into continents and islands, or even into land and
water. In Houellebecq's philosophical novel, set in what were once the Canary
Islands, the anticipated doom is not a flood; the seas have evaporated rather
than overflowed, and the Mediterranean and the Atlantic are burning deserts.
The people who vestigially linger on this parched terrain are 'neo-human'
– not unique creatures who experience everything with enraptured novelty
and store reminiscences in a private world they carry round on their shoulders,
but faint, fading off-prints from a standard prototype. A person is now an
installment in a numerical series, minimally differentiated by an Internet
Protocol and a digital address. In cyberspace, physically distinct bodies have
made way for a network of disembodied minds, plugged into each other
by go-betweens known as servers. The mutation is a corollary of ecological
change: both nationally and psychologically, islands guarantee difference, so
their obsolescence implies that the individual is defunct. When Marie22 dies
she is promptly succeeded by Marie23, who lives in 'the ruins of New York,
in the middle of what men called Manhattan', another island that has lost its
moated integrity. The Canaries were reputedly the islands of dogs, though

these fallible, short-lived creatures have been supplanted by post-canine pets. A regular-issue dog, always called Fox, dies once a decade but is immediately replaced by a cloned replica.

Daniel24, one of Houellebecq's narrators, is a Crusoe who has outlasted the apocalypse. After a further millennium of droughts and earthquakes, he lives in a compound surrounded by an electric fence, wired to deter the marauders who cluster outside. These savages are not men of another race, like Crusoe's cannibals; they are throwbacks to the old, unreconstructed model of humanity. Daniel24 neither complains about his isolation like Cowper's Selkirk nor takes arrogant pride in it like Monte Cristo. He has no need for relationships, since the desire for social commingling and physical closeness has been bred out of the renovated species. The same mutation means that he does not fall back on the unbreached security of the self, like Crusoe when he recoils from a stranger's footprint on the sand. Daniel24 refuses to define himself as a subject, because he knows that 'the subject-object separation' is a flawed by-product of the cognitive process. Tournier's Crusoe overcomes the same split when he realizes how irrelevant he is to the indiscriminately fertile life of his island. For Daniel24, that dialectical synthesis is just one more delusion: 'our status as *individuals*' is 'another name for nothingness'. He and the numbered Marys or Vincents with whom he sporadically exchanges e-mails are isolated without being dissimilar, which leaves them with no impulse to unite. Islands were once scenes of one-sided yearning: the part longs for the whole, and singleness imagines the bliss of discovering that the world, as Miranda says in *The Tempest*, has 'such people in it'. Daniel1, living in a future where procreation has been taken care of clinically, makes do with a mode of lovemaking that is contentedly insular. To masturbate, he reminds himself, is to have sex with someone you truly adore. Of course the idea is not original, because nothing is: he is unsure whether he is quoting Keith Richards, Jacques Lacan, or some other celebrity. When Tournier's

Crusoe inserts his penis into that mossy cleft, is he enjoying intercourse with nature or using the island as an aid to self-abuse? Daniel1 would choose the second option. Love, he reasons, is about fusion: this entails 'the desire for annihilation', which makes it self-murder by other means. Better to preserve your integrity by using your hand.

During a stopover at Las Palmas on his way to Lanzarote, Daniel1 has an aerial view of the Canaries. Wind brushes the dunes, and seems to be writing words or sketching human faces on the sand; the volcanic rocks look as if they have suffered torture. He is troubled by the blueness of the dwindling ocean, and thinks that it ought to be red. In a remoter future, Daniel25 reports that Lanzarote is no longer an island. For a while it was submerged, then further seismic disturbances coughed it up again; it is now an isthmus, reconnected to Africa. Daniel1 travels to the Canaries to attend a conference of the Elohimites, a religious cult whose members welcome the end of time, and organize mobs of followers to anticipate their transmigration to another world by committing suicide; immortality, according to their creed, is only granted to those who kill themselves in public. The cult's adherents, as Houellebecq whimsically pretends, include Richard Branson (who actually has designs of his own on the beyond, which he wants to make accessible for the living: in 2006 he held a press conference on Necker to announce Virgin's plans for tourism in space). Daniel1 reflects on the strangeness of the religious revival, since the Catholic faith that for centuries unified Europe like a 'massive, solid, irrefutable block' had so recently evaporated: he might be describing a continent splintering into islands that wait for their own powdery dissolution. An Elohimite elder murders an inconvenient Italian girl who has been the mistress of the cult's prophet, and justifies his act by arguing that she is just 'a pretty arrangement of particles...whose disappearance would hold no importance'. What does it matter if a coral atoll dips back below the waterline?

Before he joins in the ceremonial suicide, Daniel1 has a vision. He is dazzled by a slideshow that purports to display the design for an Elohimite embassy, shaped like a star; no building is discernible, but he sees light pulsing in waves and washing away reality until only a mystical whiteness remains. He takes this to be a preview of heaven, and understands for the first time that 'the true nature of art' is to display 'dreamed-of worlds, impossible worlds'; he has unwittingly defined the purpose of Atlantis or Utopia or Never Land or Bali-ha'i. He concludes his life by writing a poem speculating about love, that junction of bodies and souls for which neo-humans supposedly have no further need. He is not satisfied with his virtual identity, and longs to reverse the process of fission by willing Marie23 to materialize so that they can be fused. A single, unavoidable image conveys this tantalizing prospect:

There exists in the midst of time
The possibility of an island.

The only stipulation is that the island must have room for two people, rather than being the place of confinement for a solitary castaway.

The island in Daniel1's wistful poem is possible but improbable, which is why he chooses to die rather than putting his hope to the test. On our shrunken, congested globe, islands are in short supply; their scarcity announces that the imagination has stretched as far as it can go. In Saramago's *Tale of the Unknown Island*, a nameless, unnumbered king decides there is nothing left to discover, and refuses to go on subsidizing the Portuguese adventurers who sailed, like Dante's Ulysses, beyond the limits of the known world. One of the king's subjects refuses to accept the prohibition. He insists that a single unknown island remains, and requisitions a boat in which he sets out to locate it. The court philosopher invokes Donne to discredit this foolish venture; every man, he agrees, is an island – though he adds that to be truly aware of this we must transgress our own boundaries and shed the self, which only happens when we die. The journey, he predicts, will be suicidal. The crew recruited by the defiant sailor desert, weary of his quixotic crusade. But despite his misfortunes, the wish of Saramago's hero is granted. As when the Iberian peninsula secedes, magic flouts or flexes realism, and the florid language in which the tale is told brings about a small miracle. The crewless caravel is transformed by metaphor, which makes trees and plants sprout from seeds and dirt secreted on the deck; fertilized by fantasy, the vessel spontaneously blossoms. Looking like a verdant tropical island or a rootless sea-going jungle, it resumes the journey in quest of itself. Like each of us when we go on holiday, it testifies to an incorrigible optimism – bound to be disillusioned, but still reluctant to stop dreaming.

Umberto Eco's novel *The Island of the Day Before*, which might be a sequel to Saramago's fable, edges a little nearer to the unknown island. In 1643 the courtly dilettante Roberto della Griva finds himself 'shipwrecked on a deserted ship', the sole survivor of a storm. He awakens, and a mile away sees 'the form of an Island', a Platonic apparition which may actually be an undiscovered continent. A breeze ruffles its palm trees, and the conical peaks of the obligatory volcano rear in the distance. *The Tale of the Unknown Island* leaves locations unfixed, because the pursuit of an ideal can and should happen anywhere; Eco, however, quite specifically places his hero on the 180th meridian in the South Pacific. Roberto's mission, which conflates science and mysticism, is one that obsessed travellers and cabbalistic philosophers in the seventeenth century. He is taking part in a cartographic endeavour, adding vertical longitudes to the horizontal latitudes that follow the rotation of the earth. But his attempt to establish a prime meridian and to apportion time zones brings him to a fold on the map where one of the compulsory laws of physics is confounded: here the present, rather than advancing into the future, abruptly vaults backwards into the past. Eco's island lies across the notional fissure that we call the international dateline, so it is permanently becalmed in the day before today. Roberto, who cannot swim, tries to learn 'the art that would take him there', but as he paddles through the water he notices that 'the Island is receding' because of the ocean's reflux. He has to be satisfied with glimpsing an elusive place that 'by divine decree rested in the unreality, or the non-being, of the day before'. Of course this is only the belated view from west of the line. The truth about the behaviour of the islands in this limbo is even odder: if they wish, they can surreptitiously edge themselves east of the line, stealing a march on tomorrow rather than staying stalled in yesterday. In 1995 the Kiribati Islands staked a claim to the first sunrise of the twenty-first century by unilaterally nudging the dateline further east and giving Caroline Island the new name of Millennium Island. It did not enjoy primacy for long. In retaliation the King of Tonga put his island's clocks forward an hour, so as to keep ahead of Kiribati.

Hovering forever on the unapproachable horizon, Eco's island becomes a repository of magical lore. It is rumoured to be the habitat of the orange dove that announced the retreat of Noah's flood and proclaimed God's new covenant with men; it could also be a treasure island, because it lies in the vicinity of the Solomon Islands, an archipelago named in 1568 by a Spanish navigator who wanted to believe that this was where King Solomon stowed his legendary hoard of heavy gold. Roberto does not find this alchemical trove, but he chances upon another way of converting base fact into something precious or fabulous. The island is a fiction, and it turns the man who conjures it up into a romancer – or perhaps, as Eco suggests in an aside, into the first novelist. Roberto perceives that 'by inventing the story of another world, which existed only in his mind, he would become that world's master'. Eco's fantasy only needs to stretch the truth, not deny it; because fiction is always grateful for some corroborating facts, he establishes the veracity of his romance by recalling that, a few months before Roberto tried to swim to the island, Abel Tasman also sailed through that unmapped region. He, too, was hoping to bump into the Solomon Islands; he discovered Tasmania instead. In the event, that small achievement was overshadowed by a larger failure. As he sailed on, Tasman narrowly missed stumbling across the ultimate unknown island of mainland Australia, which Eco calls the 'Terra Incognita...that mankind that had been dreaming of for centuries'.

As always, my island is relegated to oblivion while the search for a larger, richer, more enticingly imaginary destination continues: better the island you don't know than one that has already been pinioned into place on the map. Tasmania has suffered the same economic distress as other islands, and now rents itself out to tourists or sedate retirees from the mainland. Emptiness, which oppressed me when I was growing up there, is its appeal for these refugees; having seen civilization, I too now understand the virtue of wilderness. But that wildness is under threat. Tasmanian politicians claim that the state's only chance of prosperity lies in the ruthless exploitation of natural resources – damming rivers or flooding alpine lakes to generate hydro-electricity, bulldozing ancient forests to produce woodchip for export to Japan. One area where the trees are being levelled and the bare ground scorched by napalm is called, morbidly enough, the Styx Valley. Though the massacre of the landscape dismays me, I cannot help remembering Daniel25's verdict – as he hikes with his cloned dog across the acrid sierra in *The Possibility of an Island* – on what he calls 'ecologism'. He looks back on the futile campaign to save the planet as 'a strangely masochistic ideology', the symptom of a self-loathing in our species: people who give prior rights to lesser animals or to trees and rivers seem to be voicing 'mankind's desire to turn against itself'. Islands are termini, and the conflicts that presage a possible end of life on earth already rage in this cul-de-sac.

To be an islander is both a privilege and an affliction; either way, the fate, like an island, sets limits beyond which you cannot move. Some people accept the world as home, others see it as a foreign place. Some of us behave as if life were an immersion, others – like me – have the sense of being stranded on a strange and vaguely inimical shore. Jung called the sense of interconnection that is meant to bind human beings together 'the oceanic feeling': we share the same element, which buoys us up. Faith of any kind, religious or political, depends on this confidence in a shared existence. Perhaps it explains the longing I always felt for cities and their erasure of personal identity, in which case it ought to reconcile me to the crush on public transport at rush hours. But the insular feeling, an aching symptom of isolation, is just as powerful. Scars tell of a recent breach; since our best option is to turn disabilities into advantages, those of us who feel this way have reason to be grateful for the wounding split that sets us apart or casts us away.

Our tiny islands, which bob like cranial eggshells on Jung's swollen ocean, give us a peculiar vantage point on the larger world; they undercut the self-importance of continents, and demonstrate that reality is not absolute or singular. There are two hundred islands in the Aegean, a thousand in the St Lawrence River, thirty-eight hundred around Japan, and up to fifty thousand off Finland. Polynesia is a synonym for innumerability, so why bother counting? At the end of the seventeenth century in his treatise on the 'plurality of worlds', the philosopher Fontenelle called the Milky Way an 'anthill of stars' and likened the constellation to the Maldives, 'those twelve thousand little islands separated merely by sea channels which one may leap almost like a ditch'. The estimate was a pardonable exaggeration: the Maldives actually consists of a mere eleven hundred islets, although Sanskrit geographers referred to the group as the Hundred Thousand Islands. Whatever the exact number, archipelagos like this are a sampling of infinitude and of inexhaustible variety. The scattered points of light or land with darkness or empty water between them testify to the value of the individual, whose private dream of an optional, irregular reality we sometimes call art. Like the seeds that Fontenelle planted in the cavernous sky, art multiplies the number of possible worlds; it designs microcosms that are often situated offshore, at the outer edge of possibility – the healing sanctuary of St Molaise or the decadent den that Monte Cristo excavates in the belly of a volcano, Prospero's magical domain or the laboratory where Moreau conducts his sacrilegious experiments, Crusoe's factory of virtuous work or Peter Pan's carefree kindergarten. There must, after all, be an island. If there were no other worlds, how could we bear to live in this one?

INDEX